"Morgan's book reveals m
written in an easily unders
owners or individuals wa.
challenges. I highly recommend *"Tax Debt Rule #1. There's ALWAYS
a Solution"*.

-Chris Hotze is the CEO of Crescere Capital and a successful real estate investor, Developer, businessman, and best-selling author of *"Mailbox Money Mindset"*

"Tax Debt Rule #1: There's ALWAYS a Solution" is a must-read for Business Owners or Individuals facing the challenges of past-due taxes to the State and Federal taxing authorities. As a business coach, I have had clients who were at times behind on taxes, which is unfortunately common in today's business community. This book will be a great resource moving forward. *"Tax Debt Rule #1: There's ALWAYS a Solution "* is filled with common-sense ideas and strategic strategies for resolving personal and business Tax Debt issues.

- William R. Maddox is the CEO and Lead Coach with Professional Performance Training Co., where he applies over 35 years of business experience to motivate, train, and inspire business owners and salespeople to meet and exceed their goals.

"The IRS Tax Codes are numerous and complex – especially for small business owners when they first start out. Business owners don't know what they don't know, so they can get ensnared in the complex web of compliance violations and penalties. Morgan's expertise provided in her book aims to help and provide business owners the resources to not only know what their options are, but to ensure they have the confidence to negotiate a reasonable solution with one of the most intimidating agencies in the world based on facts not fear. Learn why your situation is far from unique and that you are not alone by reading *"Tax Debt Rule #1: There's ALWAYS a Solution."*

-Thomas Howard is the Business Development Manager for Supporting Strategies of Merrimack Valley and is a 21+ year financial services industry professional servicing clients with banking, lending, and financial operational needs.

"Advice you receive is only as good as the person's experience giving the advice. Morgan compiled her decades of experience into written form to guide readers to make informed decisions regarding their tax health. For many readers, the dreaded notice from the Federal or state taxing authority is overwhelming and paralyzing, but inaction is not the solution. This is like receiving tragic health news, but you seek professional advice from the best physicians you can find. This is the same for the tax notices – you should seek out professionals with great experience in that specific area who understand the taxing authority. Morgan's insights will provide you with a healthy perspective so you can take proactive steps in resolving your tax situation to free you up to move forward."

- Kelly Myers provides tax, advisory, and controversary services through Myers Consulting Group LLC, employing his 40-plus years of tax experience, including over 30 years with the IRS.

"In my more than 30 years in consulting Businesses and introducing professionals who can deliver, Morgan's unparalleled expertise is a tremendous asset—her insights offer strategic tax solutions that I consistently endorse to my network. Her latest publication is the definitive guide for attaining financial clarity."

-Willie Tolbert has invested his experiences and knowledge accumulated over more than 30 years in business to create Business Resource Connector, LLC. Known as "The Guy with the Bowtie," Willie connects thousands of small business owners with the resources they need to meet and exceed their goals.

"It's about time someone revealed the secrets to successfully negotiating State and Federal past-due tax debt, and *"Tax Debt Rule #1: There's ALWAYS a Solution"* does precisely this. This book reveals many helpful strategies and industry secrets written in an easily understood manner. It is a must-read for business owners or individuals wanting a winning solution for past-due tax challenges."

-Ingrid Gee is an Internet Strategy Consultant and founder of bluedress Internet Marketing, where she applies everything she has learned in the marketing industry over the past 20+ years to a business services model that aids hundreds of clients nationwide to be a step ahead.

"Starting and running businesses creates daunting challenges, with the heightened complexity of intertwined personal and business tax strategy at or near the top of that list. As a founder of multiple businesses, Morgan's *"Tax Debt Rule #1: There's ALWAYS a Solution"* simplified and contextualized current and potential tax negotiations we are actually having. I highly recommend reading this book before or during any tax negotiations."

-Buster Arnwine is the Founder and CEO of FRG, applying his extensive experience as a Business Analyst from the last 20+ years to partner with new and growing brands to enter and expand within retail spaces.

Tax Debt Rule #1:
There's *ALWAYS* a Solution

Morgan Q. Anderson, EA
NTPI Fellow

Legal Disclaimers

This book is written to deliver accurate and authoritative information regarding the subject matter at hand. It should be understood that the author and publisher do not render legal, accounting, or tax services through this medium. The author and publisher shall not be liable for your misuse of this material. They shall have neither liability nor responsibility to anyone regarding any loss or damage caused or alleged to be caused, directly or indirectly, by the information in this book. The book is designed to inform you of the options available only. We highly recommend you seek professional advisors to assist you in determining which strategies will work in your unique and individual circumstances.

The stories of how taxpayers suffered, were about to give up, then found a solution, and now are living prosperous lives are all about real people. Some of these people are my clients; others are stories that tax resolution professionals around the country have shared with me.

The details, such as names and amounts, have been changed to protect the privacy of the individuals and their stories referenced.

Table of Content

Introduction

Having to pay taxes sucks; we all know it. However, in our country, taxes pay for our roads, schools, national defense, Social Security, and more. It's a necessary evil. When a taxpayer falls behind on their tax obligations, a dark and bumpy path begins, no matter whether an individual or a business owes the tax debt or if it's owed to the Federal or State Governments.

It doesn't matter that we are big, strong adults who carry a world of responsibility on our shoulders; having a tax debt makes the biggest and strongest of us quake in our boots. This is because the IRS and states have done a great job with the development of a reputation akin to the meanest and coldest mafia hitmen from a 1950s movie. This is intentional! They blast it all over the news when someone like Willie Nelson loses his Colorado vacation home, a local business is closed down, or Wesley Snipes goes to jail. They want you to be scared so you'll be compliant.

Yet, most tax problems happen because you got hit with some unforeseen event that put you behind the eight ball. One small disaster leads to another, and pretty soon, you're getting letters threatening to clean out your bank accounts.

Today, you have options: you can stand up to the IRS or state, and a resolution *can* be secured based on your unique financial condition.

This book will explain how the government tax collectors work and the options available to you to address past-due taxes without losing everything you have worked for. And don't worry... this book is not filled with long, drawn-out, boring tax code language that will make you fall asleep in the first two minutes. I wrote this book with the intention that it be a quick read; it's only 147 pages filled with easy-to-digest summaries of tactics that you can employ immediately and a lot of food for thought about options available.

If you do not ignore the letters and phone calls, the outcome of a negotiated resolution is far less stressful than worrying about what might happen tomorrow. The truth is that the stack of collection letters you're hiding in the bottom drawer of your desk will not go away by themselves. Luckily, there are government-sanctioned defenses and strategies to minimize the impact of tax collectors.

If you stop hiding from the debt and begin staring it right in the eye, you will realize there is *ALWAYS* a solution. You could end up addressing the debt over an extended period of time, settling for a low percentage of the total debt owed, or negotiating for the penalties to be forgiven to lowering the total balance that has to be paid back. However, you won't reach any of those options if you don't stand up and say, "I'm tired of this hanging over my head… let's get past this once and for all."

> **NOTE:** Worrying about the tax debt will cost you more in health and income than the actual collection process. You'll see a common theme in this book: everything is going to work out, because there is *ALWAYS* a solution.

In the next hour or two, you'll see how focusing on a solution to the tax debt can stop the collection letters, phone calls, and asset forfeitures by facing the tax agency head-on. You have rights that you can use to bring a final resolution to the debt.

You'll read about the strategies and inside secrets others followed when they got hit with the same unfortunate events. You will learn how the IRS and states look at your entire financial situation as a guiding point for the resolution options available.

I've outlined the strategies and variables in this book that will determine the best way to get these tax problems behind you so you can get on with your life and get the first good night's sleep you've had in a while.

Would you like to stop worrying about the tax debt and finally move on with your life? Invest one or two hours and read this book with the confidence that others have been exactly where you are and they got through it. There is *ALWAYS* a solution... let's find yours!

Chapter 1:
First Things First

A Tale of Caution

I am going to start this book with a story that hit close to home just as I began my career in late 1999... stick with me as I think it's something you should hear.

As most people in their 20s do, I was engaged in a lot of social activities to make friends. I became close to a girl named Patty, and one sunny afternoon, as we watched our dogs play in Boulder Creek, she said, "Morgan, you help people with tax debt situations, right?" When I confirmed my new line of work and shared how much I enjoyed it, she said, "I want to share something with you that I don't tell most people, but I think it is something you need to hear."

Patty told me how her father had been a big-time stockbroker on the Upper East Coast and had built a substantial fortune the family was living on. They had the big house on the shoreline with its own private beach and several boats, belonged to the "in" country and yacht clubs, and tossed money around like it was water. Unbeknownst to her Mom, Patty, and her three brothers, their financial situation was built on a house of cards.

 On Black Monday, in the biggest, most unexpected stock market crash that rocked our country, they lost everything. And with the loss of everything, a huge tax bill from the IRS would come down the pipeline at them. In the spring of 1988, when the worst of the effects from the financial crash were coming together, Patty's Dad went to a motel with a gun borrowed from a friend and committed suicide.

Patty, her three brothers, and their Mom were left to clean up the financial catastrophe. They eventually lost the house and the boats to

IRS seizures; they lost their place in the community she had grown up in and everything else about their lives that they had become accustomed to.

It was utterly devastating to Patty. She lost her father and her sense of security and had to scramble alongside her Mom and brothers to create a new normal. It was absolutely heartbreaking to hear, but it was a real-life story that has stuck with me to this day. This is why I am so passionate about my career and helping people who find themselves in a tax debt situation, like Patty's family.

I don't know what Patty's Dad was thinking when he chose to end his life over the financial losses. But this is an example of how some people can't see an end to the problem. It can feel insurmountable. It can feel like there is nowhere to turn.

I am here to tell you that there is *ALWAYS* a way to solve a tax debt issue. There is *ALWAYS* someone who can help navigate you through the twists and turns of dealing with the IRS or State and get you to the solution.

Patty's story has been the underlying inspiration that has caused me to help everyone I possibly could over the last two-plus decades I have been representing clients before the IRS and state tax agencies. It has inspired me to always let my clients know that they are not alone, that there is *ALWAYS* a solution, and that l will be their partner in identifying it and fighting like hell to negotiate it successfully.

When Ernest Hemingway was asked how he went bankrupt, he replied, "Two ways: gradually, then suddenly." That's how the IRS and states work: a letter now and then, maybe six months apart, but eventually, your name will boil up to the top of the list, and the hammer can come down hard and fast.

It's a Terrible Way to Start a Book

Reviewing an unnecessary and heartbreaking suicide is a horrific way to start a book dealing with tax debt. Trust me...personally, I agree. However, I want to convey this message to everyone with a tax debt situation, whether big or small: *NO* tax problem should ever get to the point of hopelessness. It may feel that way when looking at tens of thousands, hundreds of thousands, or even millions of dollars owed, with no idea how you will dig out from under it all. However, no matter the dollar amount, there is *ALWAYS* a solution.

Money problems drive approximately 40% of all divorces and 16% of all suicides. If that's not enough, the stress of tax debt can cause significant medical conditions, including heart attacks and cancer. No research tells us how many of those health-related fatalities had tax problems as the underlying cause, but we can guess the number is probably significant because millions of people owe past-due taxes to the IRS and state tax agencies.

Letting tax debt fester can drive you crazy with fear. Remember, the IRS and state want you to be afraid. It's not for some Machiavellian reason; it's simply because they want you to comply with your tax obligations over the fear of what *could* happen if you don't. That's why you hear about all the sensationalized IRS or state collection stories, especially around April 15th.

Living in fear over an unaddressed tax debt has a ripple effect throughout every other facet of your life: how you feel when you look in the mirror, your relationship with your partner and family, your temperament, how you sleep at night... the list goes on and on. But there is a big, sparkly light at the end of the tunnel if you only choose to face the debt head-on and get past it. Most of my clients report they are back on their feet and doing well within a few months after settling on a resolution plan to address their tax debt.

Will You Be Arrested?

This is one of the most common questions new clients ask me during our first call, so I want to address it early in this book. Going to jail over a tax debt is extremely rare. In any given year, fewer than 500 people are sent to prison; that's only 0.0000019% of all U.S. taxpayers. This figure is incredibly low when you consider the IRS found in December of 2020 that over 11.23 million taxpayers owed past-due taxes... and that's just how many they estimated owed at the Federal level!

People who do not file their tax returns or report false information may face jail time. You cannot, however, go to jail for failing to pay your taxes unless you refuse to start addressing the debt. Cheating on your taxes is a crime. Not paying your taxes if you have filed an honest return and are trying to figure out a plan to address it is not. That is why filing is so important, even if you don't have the money to pay.

> **NOTE:** Going through the resolution process is far easier if you bundle up all the years you are behind and deal with it immediately. Get the mental anguish behind you so you can get back to building your life.

The IRS Is Not as Harsh as It Used To Be

In 1997 and 1998, the IRS faced a string of legislation that flipped the collection process on its head. Previously, the IRS could aggressively pursue the collection of tax debts with little regard for due diligence. Once a debt hit the books, they would start knocking on doors and levying all available sources to collect on it with little regard for the fallout for the taxpayer.

The 1998 Restructuring and Reform Act changed things considerably. While the collection of debts was still a focus, the IRS had to follow a series of notices and required timelines before actions such as bank account levies or asset seizures could be taken. Recognition of "allowable expenses" came into play, meaning they could no longer take every penny a taxpayer had… they had to let you retain enough money to tend to you and your family's health and welfare needs. And when the IRS makes a big move like this, the states typically follow.

The taxpayer rights legislation also cleared the way for tax resolution advocates (like me) that could take the taxpayers' side. Someone to act as a buffer between overzealous collection agents and average Americans tied up in a complicated system, often through little fault of their own.

The Birth of Taxpayer Rights

Over the first 120+ years of the IRS' existence, it grew powerful and arrogant under Congress' directives with little oversight. As abuses in collections became common, Congressmen started hearing more and more horror stories from their constituents. Finally, the legislative branch realized they needed to reign in the IRS, or the system would collapse under public outcry.

Taxpayers had expressed depths of despair over their tax debt collection angst to such a degree that the government was forced to listen. The French Philosopher Montesquieu once said, "There is no greater tyranny than that which is perpetrated under the shield of the law and in the name of justice." Our Federal Government realized the error in the reckless abandon of prior IRS collection processes and reigned it in, leading the way for the states to follow suit. Today, as a result, we have sanctioned processes to follow that will allow us to work out an amicable solution if you get behind on your taxes.

The Taxpayer Bill of Rights put a lot of needed controls on the IRS when collecting past due taxes, among other things. As it stands now, taxpayers have these recognized rights:

- To be informed,
- To quality service,
- To pay no more than the correct amount of tax,
- To challenge the IRS' position and be heard,
- To appeal an IRS decision in an independent forum,
- To finality,

- To confidentiality,
- To retain representation, and
- To a fair and just tax system.

Most states followed the IRS' lead and adopted similar provisions to protect taxpayer rights.

Summary

Remember these rights if you find yourself in the crosshairs of the IRS or state. The IRS and state cannot simply bowl over you and everything you need for your health and welfare, all in the name of collecting a tax debt.

If you find that pushing back on the IRS or state scares the bejesus out of you, find an experienced tax debt resolution professional to step in as your power of attorney. They are well-schooled in your rights when dealing with the IRS and state and will make sure the line is toed.

And please remember, there is *ALWAYS* a solution. There is no reason to take drastic measures. Every single one of my past clients got their life back together and could start rebuilding their financial dreams once a resolution to address the tax debt was in place.

Chapter 2:

Sometimes Bad Things Happen to Good People

Most people who get behind on taxes do not intentionally accrue the debt. The most common way people get into trouble is when they get their return done, find they don't have enough cash to cover the tax bill, and then decide to put off filing. Or, in the case of business owners, trust the wrong in-house financial manager or borrow payroll funds to keep the business afloat.

It can take the IRS or state several years before they ask for missing returns, unlike the bank, which will start hounding you two weeks after a missed car payment. Because of this delay, taxpayers often can get lulled into a passive cocoon, figuring the tax agencies forgot about them with the hopes that no one notices.

Once you start down this path, it gets even easier to skip the next year or quarter's return and maybe the next as well. Catching up is a lot harder the longer this cycle continues; all the while, the debt owed is snowballing.

Everyone has bad luck from time to time, but the IRS and state tax collectors don't care. If you depended on this year's cash flow to cover last year's tax bills, you are thrown between a rock and a hard place if something goes wrong. And true to Murphy's Law, things go wrong when we can least afford them to.

How Do We Get Caught in the Crosshairs of the IRS or State?

Tax problems rarely start with a taxpayer's intent to stiff the IRS or state. Most tax debt cases begin with a serious life event that causes a tax issue. Tax issues can result from:

Divorce: Divorce tears apart dreams and families and can cause unpleasant tax surprises. In many divorces, the assets are liquidated to make cash disbursements. It's not uncommon for a spouse to be unaware that some property distribution payments are taxable. For example, selling your stocks to divide the cash may trigger capital gains or ordinary income tax liability. The family home sale may also create a liability.

A taxpayer may divorce near year-end and discover that taxes withheld from wages were based on filing a joint tax return with several exemptions. After filing as a single taxpayer, they find themselves grossly under-withheld and with a large, unexpected balance due. The taxpayer may be spending a lot to start over. Even amicable divorces can have these issues. When divorce turns hostile, other issues may make filing a tax return difficult. If enough animosity exists, one spouse may withhold tax documents needed to file a return or even destroy tax and business records.

Unemployment: During COVID, a young college girl who worked as a part-time waitress at my favorite restaurant got into tax trouble. She worked two nights a week and made around $150 each week. When the restaurant was forced to close, she discovered she was eligible for over $800 per week between state and federal unemployment. It was a giant gift at the time as she was able to focus on her studies and living large on weekends. But there was one sneaky detail nobody was paying attention to: the government did not withhold taxes from COVID payments.

COVID put a lot of people out of work, and the government was generous with unemployment compensation. However, they failed to tell anyone that the money could be taxed.

For those trying to get by on less income, taxes were the last thing on their mind. For people who saw their pay go up from the COVID checks, it all looked like free money, and the potential tax implications were ignored.

In the spring of 2021 and 2022, many taxpayers prepared their returns and found a tax balance due. They mistakenly believed they should not file the return for fear of the IRS or state coming down on them for the tax they could not afford. That almost always leads to a three or four-year cycle of not filing. It ends when you get calls from the IRS or state looking for the outstanding returns and payment for taxes owed.

The COVID check is a tax resolution problem we're currently dealing with on a frequent basis. It has been a few years, and the IRS and states are catching up. They stopped most collection efforts between 2020 and 2023, but the floodgates are open again, and the letters and calls are coming with a vengeance.

Taking money out of your retirement plan: When you are financially squeezed by an event outside your control and need a financial Band-Aid to get by, tapping your retirement plan seems like an easy solution if you are lucky enough to have a retirement account. However, taxes and early withdrawal penalties can leave you with one heck of a bill.

I had a client with a long-established printing company in Pennsylvania. He was a great guy who leaned on his staff to tend to a lot of the details, including having the finances overseen by his in-house accountant.

He met with the accountant weekly to review the business's financials and address any complications needing his attention. In 2006, she began telling him of a drop in profits, which caused him to pull money out of his retirement plans to infuse more capital into the business. This conversation recurred numerous times over four years, with times of reported profitability in the mix.

While his action to tap his retirement caused tax consequences, he initially could handle it. The last two years of this cycle left him with bills that could not be addressed, though he planned to address them with monthly payments as the business could afford to apply profits towards it. Little did he know that she was hiding a much bigger problem from him.

Everything came to a head when a judgment was hand-delivered to the printing company along with a demand to appear before the Commonwealth's tax board for unpaid sales taxes owed for the last four years. When the owner confronted the accountant, she admitted to hiding the debt from him but pleaded that she did so to protect him. (To keep tabs on the play-by-play of this situation, she convinced him along the way to keep diluting his financial security to put money into a business that she knew wasn't able to keep up with its taxes.)

The owner hired me to represent him and his company's interests before Pennsylvania. As I became involved with the case, something didn't feel right. I asked him if there were any other tax concerns, and though he didn't think so, he granted me Power of Attorney to look into the business tax accounts with the IRS and other state tax departments. After many calls to both, I had to tell him terrible news: payroll taxes were owed to both tax agencies, amounting to over $400,000 in addition to the sales tax debt he was already aware of. It was a nauseating situation!

Though he had tax consequences from tapping his retirement accounts, we were able to keep the aggressive collection tactics of the IRS and Pennsylvania at bay and settle on a low monthly payment plan to address the personal tax bills. For the business, the IRS and state tried to pursue the owner for personal responsibility for the taxes owed, but I was able to successfully negotiate for them to absolve him of any willful intent and redirect their pursuit to the then-fired accountant.

Debt Forgiveness: The IRS and most states tax canceled or forgiven debt. Under the cancellation of debt rules, a problem that causes an asset to be abandoned, foreclosed, or repossessed can cost taxpayers big when it comes to their annual income tax obligations. The only exception to this rule is if the taxpayer files bankruptcy.

During the collapse of 2010, a colleague of mine had a client with a $1,000,000 mortgage on his office building, which was in default. His tenants were going out of business left and right, and many had stopped paying rent. An investor offered to buy the building for $400,000 on a short sale. The bank approved the deal and forgave the loan balance, but the following January, he received a notice from the bank that the $600,000 of forgiven debt was being reported to the Federal Government. That threw him into a tax resolution case he didn't see coming.

Business Reversal: Cash-strapped business owners may pay employees their net payroll without sending the IRS or state the taxes withheld from their pay. Most business owners forced into making this type of decision initially view this as a temporary situation to preserve cash for suppliers and operating expenses. Using "tax cash" can quickly become uncontrollable.

First, the IRS and state delay detection which allows the business owner to continue the cycle without any immediate ramifications. Second, failing to remit funds to the tax agencies causes penalties and interest to accrue, worsening the issue.

The business may never recover after the IRS or state begins enforced collection. They will pursue payroll trust fund delinquencies from the

11

business as long as they are within the collection statutes that give them the right to pursue it. Additionally, they have ways to hold the responsible parties personally responsible for the debt to leverage the number of avenues they can seek the money from.

Health Issues: When you have a sick family member, taxes are not at the top of your list. Your family comes first. Yet, major health issues drain your resources, potentially leaving you unable to cover your next tax bill. Cancer or mental health issues are the types of emergency problems that no one causes, but you suffer severe consequences as you deal with them. The tax agencies may appear sympathetic, but will still pursue the tax bill.

Dicey Financial Decisions: Making the wrong judgment call when under the gun to address a financial challenge can lead to a tax debt. In our business and personal lives, many things can go wrong. One decision can often determine whether a tax debt is owed or not. I cannot tell you how often I've scrunched my forehead and thought, "Uh-oh, this isn't going to have a good ending," while listening to a client retell the story about a business decision that carried a significant tax consequence. This one topic could be 3,000 pages long. You did not set out to make a mistake; it's just that sometimes things go wrong, or you were given bad advice.

Stock Options: Non-qualified stock options can create a mess. The worst cases were in the 2000 tech stock collapse (and again several times since). Let me tell you about Gay, a California businesswoman who unknowingly and unintentionally ended up with a tax bill related to stock options. She exercised her options and made a healthy $130,000 gain, all on paper, as she did not sell the stock. She simply exercised her option to buy the stock. During the 2000 collapse, many high-tech employees were surprised that exercising options that created an on-paper profit created a tax liability.

But then the market collapsed, and her stock went to 14% of what she paid for it in January of 2000. Gay was surprised to find out that she owed taxes on stock she had bought but had not sold. By March 2000, her total portfolio was only worth about $25,000 after the collapse.

Then, she was told by her tax preparer that she owed taxes on the $130,000 gain at the time she exercised her options. The IRS wanted her to pay taxes on the gain even though she did not sell. Worse, her total portfolio was worth less than her entire tax bill.

Generally, unsold stocks are not taxable until you sell; stock options issued by your employer are handled differently.

I know it is unfair that if your stock goes up, you owe taxes on the gain, but if it goes down and you sell, you can only deduct a small portion. You can carry the loss forward and take the max deduction again next year and indefinitely. For Gay, it would be 30+ years before she could use the entire loss. If she sold, her losses were tax deductible, but only at $3,000 per year – so she will carry that loss forward for a long time.

In the meantime, she was thrown into a tax default because her phantom gains triggered an unexpected liability.

Don't Feel Embarrassed

As shown in the examples shared, most taxpayers with tax problems did not set out to "cheat the government" on their taxes.

Delinquent or unfair tax bills happen to everyone at one time or another. You are not alone. The IRS found that over 11.23 million taxpayers owed past-due taxes in 2020, and that number continues to grow every year. In 2023, the IRS reported that the tax gap, the amount of taxes owed but unpaid, was estimated to be over $688 billion as of tax year 2021… yes, that's a "B," not an "M." And this is just what has been reported by the Federal Government. Think about how many debts this equates to at the state level. Odds are, one in twenty taxpayers has a tax debt owed to either the IRS or the state.

The IRS and states may be slow, but they never forget. If you miss your car payments, 120 days later, you're taking the bus; if you miss your mortgage payment, you'll find your family sleeping at Motel 6 in about five months. But the IRS and states will let you hang yourself for two, three, or even four years (while penalties and interest pile up) before they hammer you for ALL the back taxes and additions in full, with expectations to be paid immediately.

Summary

If you have a tax debt situation, please know that you are not alone, and there is *ALWAYS* a solution! Though the IRS and state collection agents are trained to remove any semblance of personal care or sympathy from their job, you can still work with them and the parameters of the law granted to come to an amicable solution. And, if you are so inclined, bringing the right tax debt resolution professional into the negotiation battlefield to fight for your rights and leniency whenever and wherever possible will ensure you get the best solution possible.

When I look back on the thousands of clients I have helped over the last two-plus decades, I see tons of good people who unintentionally got in trouble with the IRS or the state. Even those who have made mistakes but want to fix their tax issues deserve compassion and a second chance. In this book, I will outline what can be done to address your tax debt. I hope you find it to be the helping hand you need to finally address your tax debt concerns once and for all!

Chapter 3:

The Inside Secret of the Tax Agencies and the Dreaded Audit

> **NOTE:** First things first, if you receive a letter from the IRS or state advising that you are being audited, DO NOT IGNORE THIS LETTER!!!!

When your tax return is flagged for review, you will be notified of an audit via the mail in one of those envelopes with the return name and address we have all been trained to dread. However, don't let your fear get the better of you! This first notification is them trying to "play nice." They found an anomaly on your tax return that they want to investigate. It starts innocent enough...

If the IRS does not receive a response from you within 30 days of the initial contact letter, they will issue another letter containing a bit stronger language that points out the areas of concern and provides another deadline to respond. If you do not respond again, a notice of deficiency will be issued. At this point, you can request a reconsideration of the audit determination or challenge the determination by filing suit in the United States Tax Court. While each state handles audits differently, they follow a similar path to the IRS. You will be one step ahead if you understand how the IRS and states work and what motivates the initial flagging of a tax return for review.

The common triggers that open a review of your taxes are:

1. You failed to file your return.

2. Your return has errors, and the tax agency wants it fixed.

3. They believe you are underreporting your income.

4. Expenses claimed seem exorbitant.

5. Questionable deductions were claimed.

Now, there is one more, and it can feel the most offensive: a third party can report you to the IRS or state for nefarious claims made by you or your business on tax returns. This is known as the Whistleblower Program by the IRS and typically carries similar titles with the states. Anyone can call the IRS or state and report that they know you falsified documentation, did not claim income, or claimed deductions on your tax returns that you didn't qualify for. It might even be one of those buddies down at the bar who heard you bragging about 'under the table' income and were jealous of your success.

We've also seen cases where a disgruntled employee, ex-spouse, or business partner called in a tip to the tax agencies, causing a can of worms to be opened. Though the assertions made by the whistleblower may not be factual, you will be guilty until you prove yourself innocent. Though some of the IRS and state's open cases come from whistleblower claims, I would venture to guess that 99.9% come from what was, and sometimes more importantly, what *wasn't* claimed on a return.

Many tax account issues start with a failure to file or underreported income, closely followed by an audit of past returns. Audits can be extremely uncomfortable to work through, which is the intention of the IRS and states. Again, they "encourage" voluntary compliance with tax laws; anything perceived as a taxpayer stepping outside the expected boundaries is a place where the IRS and state want you to be uncomfortable.

I am the first person to say that decisions you make regarding how you report your financial activities on the tax return carry consequences. And, as an Enrolled Agent licensed by the Federal Government to represent taxpayers, I have an ethical obligation to tell you that you should follow the tax codes to the "T." That being said, there are gray areas in our tax code. You can't possibly be expected to be a saint on your annual tax return, but you most certainly don't want to be a sinner.

In 2018, a colleague had a new client undergoing an IRS audit. The client swore that the worst his audit could get was the IRS determining he would owe another $50,000 in tax. A year later, the number was $170,000 because the taxpayer could not stop oversharing about his circumstances and nefarious financial activity reporting during the audit meetings.

For no reason at all, during the audit interview, he volunteered that he took his family with him to a business conference in Hawaii that he wrote off on his tax return, including the extra five weeks there when he wasn't in meetings. Then, he mentioned they rented their home out on Airbnb, talked about a net loss carry forward from years ago, and his accelerated depreciation tactics.

I was not in the room during the audit, having only heard the tale of the hearing from my colleague, though I wish I had been!!! Auditors are trained to get you talking in hopes that you will give them clues on how to extract more money from you. I know the traps that get laid and have become an expert at navigating the chessboard silently used during an audit hearing.

Rule Number One If You Find Yourself In an Audit

Remember the number one rule during an audit meeting: **keep your mouth closed until you are asked a pointed question. Then, answer in the most straightforward manner that sufficiently addresses the question.** If possible, try to complete the audit via correspondence instead of through a telephone or in-person hearing. An audit inquiry can often be addressed by providing the documentation requested with a basic explanation.

Here is a cautionary tale about audits:

Sarah ran a small business in Colorado out of her house as a talent broker for businesses. As a recruiter, she matched people searching for jobs with local companies with spots to fill. Sarah developed a decent-sized business providing these services, grossing around $220,000 annually and clearing a net profit of $125,000.

Her net was high because she ran the business out of her house, allowing her to be home with her children. She triggered an audit because her advertising budget was 35% of her gross. Red flags pop up in the IRS and state databases whenever an expense appears out of the normal range for a small business. Recruiters typically spend around 35% of their gross income on advertising, but the IRS' audit flag rules aren't always accurate or current.

The audit started as a correspondence audit, simply looking for the receipts and proof of the 35% advertising cost, but the auditor decided to conduct a phone interview as well. During the interview, the auditor said, "I used to run a business out of my home; I loved it because the kids could play in the corner of the room while I got my work done." She said it in such a friendly mom-to-mom voice that Sarah replied, "Yes, I have a big window in my office with lots of light, and the kids often play board games or work on their iPads in the corner."

The advertising deductions remained intact when the audit report came in from the IRS a few months later. However, the $6,800 Sarah had deducted for home office use was disallowed. The report stated that the office in the home was not used *exclusively* for the business; this was because of Sarah's disclosure that the kids often played in the room.

Just one voluntary statement made in a friendly manner, and Sarah ended up owing around $3,000 in taxes, interest, and penalties. This is just one of the reasons you should never handle an audit on your own.

Sarah would have paid my office or her tax preparer about $1,000 to conduct the audit but chose to handle it on her own and ended up having to pay the IRS an additional $3,000.

Oh, and one more thing. Audit results are shared with the state. Since Colorado has an income tax, Sarah got another notice about six months later asking for $500 more, including the penalties and interest, in state income tax for the disallowed home office deduction.

When Sarah contacted our office about the tax bills and if there was any way to challenge them, I was honest with her. I told her to pay the tax bill because going to war with the IRS over a small amount like this is not worth the cost of professional representation. When faced with a small tax bill, it is wise to seek qualified advice from someone who can give you a clear picture of the cost of the battle and the chances of winning.

Why Is the Tax Code So Complicated?

In an era of tremendous partisan conflict on nearly every issue, there is one conviction that Democrats, Republicans, and independents all share: the American tax code is a disaster. But interestingly, it is our own fault.

Economists and tax professionals have long criticized the tax code's complexity as wasteful, inequitable, and ripe for evasion. As reported by the Pew Research Center in April of 2023, 53% of U.S. adults report that the complexity of the code is a problem for them. Policymakers from both parties have talked about replacing the current tax code with a more straightforward, easier-to-understand method for raising revenue.

Nonetheless, despite adjustments at the margins by the Biden, Trump, and Obama administrations, this uniquely American tax system endures and isn't going away anytime soon. There are various causes for this, including political posturing, policy inertia, and lobbying influence over tax policy, to name a few. But, oddly enough, the fundamental reason is that the public wants it that way, despite our protests about complexity and unfairness. *We love our deductions.*

The government wants you to own a home, save for retirement, invest in businesses, adopt needy children, and even build apartment and office buildings. They encourage the desired behavior through the tax code to incentivize you to do what the government has decided would be best for America.

Providing incentives through the tax code to get the desired outcome is more popular than just writing checks to citizens. Politicians need to get re-elected, so they often take the easy way out and highlight our tax system as "broken" and "something we are dedicated to fixing." Who wouldn't jump on that bandwagon??? Unfortunately, it never happens because it's a giant, convoluted, three-eyed monster with too many beneficial loopholes that most don't want to be changed.

After your tax debts are cleared up, if you aren't working with a tax return preparer that you are comfortable with, I can connect you with someone vetted who can work with you to leverage your financial condition in the most tax-advantageous way possible. Again, you don't want to be a "sinner," but you shouldn't be a "saint" to your own detriment by not incorporating tax planning accordingly!

Dealing with the IRS or state can be perplexing and complicated. The tax agencies wield considerable power, but you have rights if you ask for them, even during the audit process.

The Various Audit "Flavors"

The IRS or state will pursue different types of audits, each leaving a different taste in your mouth when they are finished. The three most common types of audits are:

The Correspondence Audit

I think of this type of audit as "the spoiled milk audit." Nobody likes the smell or taste of it, but you move past it pretty quickly.

The correspondence auditing program is expanding with the IRS, especially since COVID, and the states are following suit. In the initial letters, the IRS or state will ask questions about specific items on the tax return, such as income, expenses, and itemized deductions. The taxpayer should respond to the letter in a timely fashion, which typically means within a few weeks. These are the least intimidating types of audits as they rarely progress further as long as you submit everything requested and are thorough with your response.

The In-Office Audit

I associate this flavor of audit with "burning the roof of your mouth from piping hot pizza cheese." It stings, and you're going to feel it for several days, but it eventually goes away.

For this type of audit, you will receive correspondence requesting you to report to the local IRS or state office on a specific date and time. The letter provides a list of the documentation the agent wants you to bring for their review and comparison to the return filed; it usually means that a significant discrepancy or concern has been found that warrants a more involved review.

My experience has been that many times, you can get these converted to correspondence audits if you call to advise that you are unavailable to appear that day and offer to send copies of the documentation requested. You can follow up on this request with a commitment to speak with the agent after they review the documents submitted to review any questions or clarifications they may need. Since COVID, we have found that most IRS and state-level agents are amenable to this change in their audit processes.

The Field Audit

This is the most invasive type of audit and is typically reserved for business-related audits. I refer to this one as a "5-alarm ghost pepper hot sauce that causes ulcers and stomach pangs for months."

This audit begins with a notification that the IRS or state will be at your home or office on a specific date to review your financial records for the specified tax year or period. Get out your diving suits and oxygen tanks because this will be the deepest dive into your financials you have ever seen.

The IRS or state will send a team to your location and ask for office space or a dedicated room to conduct the review, which means your personal or business space might be tied up for a week or more. They will ask you to help directly or to provide someone who can find documents, make copies, answer questions, etc. If the audit is for your business, it disrupts your operations. Plus, a room full of IRS or state agents is scary to everyone in the company, and rumors will more than likely fly. It is always best to involve a professional representative for a business audit as they are tricky to handle.

The Taxpayer Compliance Measurement Program

There is one more type of audit explicitly conducted by the IRS that is not initiated by anything the taxpayer reports: the Taxpayer Compliance Measurement Program audit (also referred to as a TCMP audit). There is no "flavor" to this one… it happens rarely, and it just plain sucks. While this type of audit has a true and defendable purpose, those unlucky enough to be chosen are put through the wringer.

The IRS uses the TCMP audit to determine the baseline for compliance with the tax codes and deductions afforded to taxpayers. It helps establish the averages for business expenses or charitable contributions and general compliance. The IRS uses the TCMP audits to continue building and assessing the average taxpayer's compliance and framework for average deductions claimed, which is used as a basepoint for all taxpayer returns moving forward.

It's strictly a random event if you get picked, and unfortunately, it is one of the most involved types of audits because they ask taxpayers chosen to prove ALL income and ALL deductions or expenses claimed. The audit is so cumbersome that legislation has been considered (but never passed, of course) to compensate the 'victims' with a $3,000 tax credit.

As mentioned above, these audits are rare; however, I wanted to tell you about them in case you fall into the unlucky group of taxpayers chosen.

They Already Know 95% of What You're Doing

In my experience, auditors rarely ask a question they don't already know the answer to. That's because of the Information Returns Processing (IRP) system. This Federal database receives information submitted by employers, banks, 1099's, and other third parties (payers like Visa and Venmo) reporting taxpayer financial activities such as transfers, payments, wages, pensions, interest earned, and dividends paid during the tax year.

The IRP process begins with the Federal Government receiving approximately five billion monthly reports on money movement. These wage and non-wage information documents are then processed and prepared for computer matching with individual or business income tax returns.

It takes the IRS, on average, 17-24 months from the time they begin to receive returns until the non-filer and under-reporter notices are sent to taxpayers. The match identifies cases in which taxpayers under-reported their income on tax returns or did not file returns at all. This is why it can seem that the IRS takes years to catch up with an error on your tax return.

Remember that about 95% of the economy is tracked electronically. When the auditor asks questions about assets at the beginning of your encounter, they know most of the answers. My belief from having been involved with hundreds of audits over the years is that they want to discover upfront if you will try to hide assets or income.

I know your friends probably tell you about the under-the-table income they receive and how they scammed the IRS and state, but you should know that most of that is barroom talk. The downside of IRS or state problems are not worth the 25% in taxes you'll save on a few hundred here or there. Be honest and stay off the radar. There are plenty of ways to reduce your taxes that are IRS and state approved.

> **NOTE:** Once again, keep your mouth shut if you have pushed the envelope and are under audit. The more you talk, the bigger the hole you can dig without even trying. Get someone like me to handle the agent interview for you.

Some Correspondence Audits Are Big

A few years ago, a colleague of mine had a client whose corporation was domiciled in Wyoming (a good state for asset protection), but the owners lived 1,000 miles away. In 2014, they had one heck of a great year and reported a profit of 2.4 million, about 10x more than the average income for the past six years. That must have been enough to trigger an audit, as the letter came in 2017. In the meantime, those 2014 profits were good enough to hit the client's "we've done enough, let's move on" number, and they started winding down the business and moved to Arizona to retire.

Normally, the audit would have been moved to the Arizona office, but the auditor in Wyoming did not appear to want to give up the big case. While auditors aren't paid on commission, they have performance quotas, and promotions can consider their examination case log and results. This case was more extensive than most, so I'll let you make your assumption here.

The Wyoming auditor requested an 'in-office' audit, meaning the client was being asked to travel back to Wyoming for an undetermined amount of time to go through the review process. The client contacted the Wyoming CPA that compiled their return for assistance, but he declined, stating that he was too consumed with his current caseload to provide the assistance necessary.

My colleague was brought into the case by referral and immediately contacted the auditor to see if he could keep the client from traveling back to Wyoming. He successfully negotiated a deal where he would not protest the audit being done in Wyoming if they could transition it to a correspondence audit so everything could be done by phone, fax, and mail. He also insisted that all communications were done through his office and that the taxpayers would only be brought in if it was absolutely necessary.

One of the significant advantages of a correspondence audit is that it's harder to say something that can lead to even more problems than were initially of concern to the IRS or state.

Though the audit required the submission of several rounds of documentation and several phone calls to discuss items of concern or address questions the Auditor had, everything was brought to a close with minimal tax consequences and without the taxpayer ever having to speak with the auditor directly.

Few people realize that you can negotiate a venue change with the IRS or state, especially if you understand the needs of the auditor or collection agent. As long as the auditor can secure the records and information needed to assess the reported financial activities accurately, it can save taxpayers a lot of downtime from their business or family. And if a professional is involved, the taxpayer can even be spared from having to speak directly to the auditor.

Typical Correspondence Audits Are Simple To Address

Most correspondence audits are not that big. Most are simple questions about a line item on your return. They are pretty straightforward. Initially, the IRS or state will send a letter to the taxpayer requesting information or explaining corrections and seeking the taxpayer's agreement to the adjustments.

This happens a lot for businesses when expenses, such as travel and entertainment expenses or advertising, are higher than other businesses in similar industries.

> **NOTE:** Save your documents. Today a scanner is so cheap, and online storage is almost free – it pays to just save everything. If you're wondering how long you should save documents, the required answer is seven years, but it's never a bad practice to keep your records for ten years.

So, if they ask why you spent so much money on marketing, you will need to send in copies of your contracts with the vendors and any supporting information you can find, such as a picture of an ad that ran or a copy of a sales flyer.

If you are advertising online through an avenue like social media, print the reports from the Facebook ad manager. Then, include a short letter explaining why it is customary for a business of your type to spend so much on getting new customers.

A no-change letter will be issued if the taxpayer's audit response to the IRS or state addresses any concerns satisfactorily. Something simple like this can be handled directly by you without involving a tax professional.

If the IRS or state requires additional information, they will request it in writing. If the second explanation does not resolve the issue, the return may be forwarded to a local office for further review. Or, if the taxpayer's information is not satisfactory to the IRS or state, a letter informing the taxpayer of proposed tax changes and appeal rights will be issued.

The job of a tax professional when it comes to a correspondence audit is to prevent anything from going south and to figure out how to keep it from being shifted to an in-office or in-the-field audit. Those types of audits are costly because of how much time a professional needs to be involved to handle them. Still, it is usually worth your peace of mind knowing that your position is defended in the most beneficial and thorough way possible.

Do You Have To Turn Over Your Accounting Software?

A favorite new trick is to ask for your QuickBooks backup files. You'll hear how this expedites the audit: "We can close your case quicker." Please don't believe it! You do not have to provide all of your financial information and raw data unless you are subpoenaed for it. Letting the IRS or state dig around in your financial affairs for three years is a good way for them to find little things that can lead to more significant problems. Say "no," or let a professional say "no" for you.

Send Copies, Not Originals

Never, *ever* send the IRS or state original documents. Always send copies, and make sure to send all correspondence via certified mail with a return receipt requested. The auditor will ask you to fax the documents but politely ask for an address you can mail them to instead. This gives you verifiable confirmation that your documents arrived, as the IRS and states have occasionally lost documents and held the taxpayer responsible. I know it's unfair, but you must play the game by their rules.

One More Story

Remember, you may ignore a money-in event, especially cash, but there is a good chance the transaction was recorded and tracked somewhere. Small transactions can slide under the radar, but let me tell you about a client who did handyman work on the weekends that caused a tax audit and problem.

Chris worked hard every Saturday, fixing little things for people in his neighborhood. He always asked for cash. So far, so good; but then he made a bad judgment call and began deducting his expenses for that side business on his annual income tax return, which triggered an audit. A few red flags popped up when Chris tried deducting small equipment and supplies expenses against a business with zero revenue.

Most auditors have seen hundreds of cases similar to Chris' during their tenure with the IRS or state, his auditor being one of them. Based on the expenses claimed, even though no income records were on paper, estimated income was assumed.

Now, I'm going to throw in a HUGE disclaimer here: I'm not telling you to cheat on your tax returns or not claim side income earned. However, Chris could have handled his situation much differently to stay out of trouble. If he wanted to stay off the radar of the IRS, he could have absorbed his handyman expenses and forgotten about the tax deductions. Then, when he collected that $300 or $400 every Saturday in cash, he could have used it to pay for entertainment, gasoline, and groceries.

The Final Word

DO NOT CHEAT. Do not mix your personal expenses with your company bank accounts. Please do not buy a big screen T.V. for "office use," then install it at home to be enjoyed by your family. The real problem with cheating is that it makes you think like a cheater, and it is hard to control dishonest behavior if we normalize it. Plus, who can sleep at night worrying about the IRS or state second-guessing everything?

If you have pushed the envelope in the past, keep your mouth shut. But I strongly suggest you walk the straight and narrow moving forward.

Summary

The IRS and state know 95% of what goes on in America because they get billions of reports about the movement of your money. That is why they know if you don't file a return or under report your income.

When the computer system flags your return for review, you start getting letters. Some can be solved in one phone call or a simple exchange of correspondence, while others drag on for a year or more, especially if you're in a complicated business situation.

When you're in the line of fire of an auditor, they have two main objectives.

1. To make sure you are charged as much tax as they can legally assess, and

2. To get your case closed quickly.

Your objective is to remove the emotional stress of dealing with the IRS or state by being prepared while doing everything possible to ensure tax problems do not disrupt your life. Whatever audit you are faced with, it is always best to prepare and remain calm. Remember, there is *ALWAYS* a solution to any tax problem encountered.

Chapter 4:

Payroll Tax Debts and Pitfalls to Be Aware Of

For those of you who have employees and the responsibilities that go with them, this chapter is dedicated to you.

Whenever you have employees, you have the obligation to withhold taxes from their paychecks and turn that money over to the IRS and state for income tax, Social Security, Medicare, and any state tax that employees are required to contribute to. Because of this required transaction every payroll, the governments dub these monies as trust taxes: you take the tax money out of your employee's paychecks and hold it *in trust* to turn over to the IRS and state.

The business is required to submit these tax payments on a set schedule throughout the year, depending on how many employees you have, the gross payroll amounts, and the frequency with which you distribute payroll. At the onset of your business operations, you should have reviewed your requirements with your accountant or payroll service provider to understand these filing and payment requirements clearly.

Even if you did your due diligence at the onset of your business and learned your filing and payment obligations, things happen, and payroll taxes accrue! In my experience, the most common causes of the beginning of a payroll tax problem are:

- Being stiffed by a client – I have had clients who were owed tens and sometimes hundreds of thousands of dollars for work

31

performed that they could never recoup. This could be because their client went out of business unexpectedly, their client died and there was no way to recover the money owed, bad contracts that left loopholes for my client not to be paid, and even having their customers file bankruptcy with other debts that superseded my client's rights to be paid.

- Internal theft – This one is always a tough pill to swallow because trusted individuals take nefarious actions within a client's organization that leave the company in dire straits. To make it worse, I would estimate that 60% of the time, the theft is committed by a trusted family member.

- Natural disasters such as hurricanes, tornados, fires, etc. - The financial disruption caused by a natural disaster is far-reaching, and most business owners do not have sufficient insurance to cover business disruptions. The physical impact of a natural disaster on equipment, vehicles, and inventory can be bad, but when, for example, a tornado hits an entire area, work can come to a grinding halt for months.

- Unexpected business loss – I have had clients who invested in additional high-dollar equipment and brought additional employees on based upon a pending contract with a customer, and then the customer decided not to proceed. I have had clients put out of business due to new competition that offered similar services or products at a cheaper rate.

Whatever your situation, please know that you are not alone! In 2021, it was estimated that over 22% of small businesses owed past-due taxes to the IRS. Given that there were 32,540,953 registered small businesses in the US in 2021, that means millions of small businesses had past-due tax bills. And if you are reading this book, consider yourself ahead of the fray because most of them aren't being proactive in finding a solution to the tax debt.

Why the IRS and States Bare Their Teeth Over Payroll Tax Debts

Why the IRS and States Bare Their Teeth Over Payroll Tax Debts

There are two reasons the IRS and states jump all over payroll tax debts:

- The *trust* factor: your employees are getting paid less than their gross income with the belief that you are paying the withheld monies to the government on their behalf.

- The annual filing factor: when your employees get their W-2 from you at the end of the year, they file their income tax returns based on the information reported on that document. For most hard-working W-2 employees, when they fill out their 1040 claiming their spouse, children and all the deductions they qualify for, they are usually owed a refund. *The IRS and states will never refuse to issue a refund to a W-2 employee simply because the employer failed to submit the withheld payroll taxes.* As such, the IRS and states lose out on positive cash flow whenever an employer does not pay over the withheld taxes.

Remember that the IRS and state collection departments are only as good as the databases they get their information from, so you won't hear from them immediately. This is why a business with cash flow issues typically has a runaway tax debt by the time the IRS or state catches onto the situation and pesters the business to address it.

Businesses always have a slew of bills that need to be tended to: inventory, supplies, utilities, fuel, etc. When things get tight, those items must be paid or the business' ability to function is paralyzed. Business owners do everything they can to prevent it, but not paying a payroll tax can make perfect sense when push comes to shove. The power isn't going to be turned off if the payroll tax payment isn't addressed, but it will be if the electric bill isn't paid. The next customer's roof won't be impacted if the payroll tax payment isn't addressed, but it will be if the shingle supplier isn't paid. It's very easy to see how a payroll tax issue begins. The thought is typically, "I may not be able to pay it now, but I've got a big job coming up next month and can use those funds to catch up."

Unfortunately, the catch-up never happens. And once a business owner realizes that the IRS hasn't reached out for several weeks, and even months, about unpaid payroll taxes owed, it becomes an easy avenue to "rob Peter to pay Paul."

How Can Unpaid Payroll Taxes Be Addressed?

Remember, there is *ALWAYS* a solution! The IRS and states typically employ the same resolution options for a business' unpaid taxes as they do for individuals. Though all states have different resolution programs and rules, they usually follow options similar to the IRS. And with the IRS, you can even submit an Offer in Compromise to address an unpaid business payroll tax!

I would caution you to work with an experienced tax professional if you have a business with payroll tax debt. The IRS and states are more critical of unpaid payroll taxes than an individual's unpaid income tax, so more moving parts come into play. This is where personal responsibility for a business payroll-related tax debt is a factor that you need to be sensitive to. The IRS refers to it as the Trust Fund Recovery Penalty (TFRP), with most states having a similar monicker.

What Is the TFRP?

The Trust Fund Recovery Penalty (TFRP) or similar state penalties are personal assessments against the individual(s) responsible for overseeing a business withholding payroll taxes from employee paychecks without ensuring those tax monies were paid to the IRS or state. It's a way for them to pierce any corporate veil and leverage the repayment of the taxes owed from multiple sources.

Is this legal? Yes, 100% yes.

For a sole proprietor, there is no such thing as a personal assessment because the individual and the business are viewed as one and the same.

However, personal assessments for unpaid payroll tax obligations related to LLCs, partnerships, non-profit organizations, and corporations can be made.

Exposure to these assessments doesn't stop with just the business owner. Here's a list of who can potentially be held personally responsible for the payroll taxes not being paid over to the government:

- Business Owners
- CEOs and CFOs
- Directors and Managers
- Third-party Payroll Providers
- Accountants or Bookkeepers
- Board Members
- Trustees
- Shareholders, and more

As you can see, the IRS and states will look at a wide range of potentially responsible parties to see if they can leverage their collection reach into more pools of opportunity.

> **Here's a tidbit to remember:** trust taxes can never be discharged in a Bankruptcy. It doesn't matter if a business files bankruptcy protection with outstanding payroll taxes or if an individual files it with TFRP or payroll-related personal assessments. They will not just be "forgiven" through bankruptcy.

Determining Personal Responsibility

As uncomfortable as it may sound, an investigation for personal responsibility assessments begins when an unaddressed payroll tax debt is on the books with the IRS or state and the business can't quickly pay the debt in full. Typically, two phrases guide these investigations: who was "willful" and who could be "responsible" for the payroll taxes going unpaid. Though every state handles these investigations a bit differently, these phrases are the key to holding someone accountable and can sometimes be the key to getting someone out of the crosshairs of the IRS or state.

Usually, the IRS and state will interview all parties who could be held accountable to determine their roles within the organization and the tasks each was responsible for. They will ask for bank account records to see who was signing the business checks and who had debit cards issued to them for the business bank accounts. They will pull copies of the registration paperwork recorded with the Secretary of State to see who was listed on all the organizational paperwork. They will check to see whose John or Jane Hancock is on the tax returns. They will look in every direction possible to expand the collection opportunities.

So, What's the Best Way To Handle This Situation?

First and foremost, as mentioned above, the IRS and state will be more aggressive about unpaid payroll taxes than any other tax type accrued; therefore, you want to be proactive. Don't hide unopened notices from the IRS or state in the back of your desk drawer. Don't leave phone messages left by Revenue Officers or Collection Agents unanswered. If you ignore it, your business will be more susceptible to aggressive collection tactics such as field visits to your office or job sites, bank account levies, or levy orders issued to your customers.

If, for example, you come to me with payroll tax problems, my first step will be to talk to the Revenue Officer or Collection Agent and explain that you are aware of the tax debt issue, you have brought me on board to seek a solution to the problem, and that our priority will be the current tax obligations that need to be tended to. We have to stop the bleeding, so focusing on the current payroll's tax obligation is our numero uno priority! Upon hearing this introduction, most Revenue Officers and Collection Agents pause and take a deep breath. They know that with those words, you are drawing a thick line in the sand with your responsibilities.

Once we prove that a current payroll tax obligation payment is tended to, we will ask for a 30 to 60-day collection hold on the account. This timeframe will be used to pull together a complete financial picture of the business that will serve as justification for the resolution we propose, whether that be a monthly repayment plan, an Offer in Compromise, or any other sanctioned option.

Remember, when dealing with the IRS and states, the priority is to stop any additional taxes from being added to the bill. The Revenue Officer or Collection Agent may throw their weight around a bit and demand higher monthly payments towards the bill than you can afford, or we propose, but they will never push a business to pay an amount every month that will put the ongoing tax compliance in jeopardy.

The 1099 Vs. W-2 Issue

There are hard and fast rules behind classifying a worker as a contractor versus an employee. Look this topic up on the internet, and you will find pages of articles about the ins and outs of these designations. You can't go back in time to change a designation. If the topic hasn't come up yet with the IRS or state, do your due diligence now and make sure you have your workers classified correctly moving forward by checking out the IRS questionnaire, Form SS-8.

Suppose you've been questioned by the IRS or state about the contractor classification for your workers. The IRS tells you to convert to W-2s and start withholding taxes. You have three choices:

A) Close your business and quit (which I don't recommend because there is *ALWAYS* a solution).

B) Comply and hire a payroll company today.

C) Ask for an administrative hearing and convince the judge that your people are correctly classified as 1099 contractors.

Most businesses get caught in this headache through complaints from their workers. Imagine I'm a roofer on one of your crews and made $75,000 last year. Suddenly, the IRS wants $15,000 for income and self-employment taxes to cover Social Security and Medicare. I'm not going to blame myself for failing to hold a little back each month for the taxes; I am going to lay 100% of the blame on you, even if you had me sign an agreement saying that I agree to be a 1099-classified worker. And even if you reviewed my tax obligations with me ten times. The IRS will follow up on the complaint, and if it is found that I was incorrectly classified as a 1099 contractor, you will be on the hook.

This is a nightmare scenario because the IRS can ask you to pay what should have been paid for the payroll taxes, not just for the current quarter, but going back to when the workers first should have been classified as employees. You won't be able to ask for those tax monies back from your workers, so you will be stuck with a large tax bill to fund. Additionally, penalties could be assessed up to 100% of the unpaid taxes that *should* have been paid. The final cherry on top is the interest that will be tacked onto the unpaid tax and penalties assessed. It's a tough situation for a business to absorb financially.

Summary

Payroll taxes are nothing to slough off with. They are challenging to address, impossible to bankrupt out of, and the IRS will come after you with both barrels loaded. Of all the tax debt types that I caution anyone to pay the most attention to, this is the biggest.

But, as I've already said multiple times in this book, there is *ALWAYS* a solution. I recommend that you engage an experienced tax debt resolution professional to help. There are too many moving parts to a payroll tax situation that prevents a DIY attempt from being reasonable.

Chapter 5:

Should I Feel as Threatened as I Do by the Notices I Get from the IRS and State?

The notices the IRS and state send out for past-due tax debts are *meant* to be intimidating. They are designed to get your attention and intimidate you enough that you start throwing any available monies toward the debt as quickly as possible so you stop receiving them.

It can *feel* like every single notice that hits your mailbox from the IRS or state is a precursor to them busting down your door and doing everything to collect on the debt, including taking your first-born child, but that's not the case. When you see the envelope sitting in your mailbox with the IRS or state tax agency return address in the upper-left-hand corner, I know that dread shivers up your arm, but it doesn't need to.

Remember, there is *ALWAYS* a solution.

The Source of Those Ugly Notices

The IRS and states mostly use computer-generated bills and notices to communicate with taxpayers about any issues on a tax account. Parameters are set in their computer systems to identify potential issues or balances owed on accounts, which trigger a series of notices to be timed and released. Until a release code is noted on the account (in most cases, meaning a payment is made), the notices automatically get sent to you.

Now, it has been suggested on the internet that 1 in 4 notices triggered by the IRS system is wrong. I have not found that to be the case based on the hundreds of thousands of notices I have received and addressed for my clients over the decades I have been in practice, but I have found errors from time to time.

> **NOTE:** Just because you receive a notice from the IRS or state, it doesn't necessarily mean it's correct. Don't panic! Remember, there is *ALWAYS* a solution!

Why do they keep using the computer-generated notice system if it has the potential for errors? Because it works! The average first-level bill sent out by the IRS is usually under $1,000. Most law-abiding citizens will assume that the IRS records must be correct and simply pay the bill.

For taxpayers like you with larger liabilities that can't be addressed by simply stroking a check for a couple of hundred dollars, the system-generated notices are an effective way for the IRS and state to chase the debt. Before specific collection actions can be taken on a past-due tax debt, a series of notices and final demands must be issued first. It is cost-effective for the IRS and states to use computers to issue those notices instead of paying the salaries of the thousands of people it would take to generate those notices manually.

The Most Common Notices Issued

The IRS and states have hundreds of notice and letter variations to address tax account issues. In 2022, it was estimated the IRS issued over 150 *million* notices. So, if you received a few, count yourself as the tiniest of blips on the IRS' radar screen, but don't ignore them!

The following are summaries of the most common types of notices issued:

Math errors: The IRS or state claims your tax return contains math errors. For example, you listed three children for the refundable tax credit but only provided two names and tax identification numbers. That is going to change your credit/refund. The computer system will make the automatic correction and issue a notice about the changes made. Slow down and read the notice fully to ensure the correction was needed and that the "correction" wasn't an error to your detriment.

Penalty notices: If you fail to file on time or make a payment by the deadline, the system will automatically calculate a penalty and ask you to pay the amount due. Before you make a payment to address the penalty charge, make sure their assessment is correct. I have had clients who have received penalties for the late filing of a return, though they had proof it was submitted on time. You can write a letter back to the office that sent you the notice, attach a copy of the notice, and ask for the penalty to be abated.

Interest assessments: Late payments on any tax bill will generate automatic interest-due notices. You will also receive updated balances on unpaid tax debts that reflect the continuing interest accrual.

Underreported income: This is the big one that warrants your immediate attention. The IRS typically leads the charge with this type of situation and then notifies the correlating state of any changes to taxable income deemed appropriate.

Here's how this works: whenever an income tax return is filed with the IRS, the computer system matches the amount of income reported with all wage and income records provided in the form of 1099s and W-2s. This notice will be issued if there is a discrepancy in the government's favor. "You reported gross income of $160,000, but we have reports that you received $210,000. As such, we have assessed additional taxes to your account, and you have a balance due." The most common cause for this issue is a missed 1099.

Remember, the IRS knows about 95% of what happens in the economy, and your debits and credits are someone else's credits and debits. That means when someone gave you money, they recorded it as an expense. The problem is that the numbers may not always match, or you recorded the income or expense in a different spot than the IRS expected. If they think something is wrong, they bill you for the additional tax and let you prove otherwise.

What To Do If the Notices You Receive Are Flat-Out Wrong

First, pay the bill if the balance is under $500 and you don't have the time or inclination to fight it. I know that sounds ugly... it feels ugly to say! However, the reality is that it could cost more in aggravation and time than the balance reflected on the notice. Hiring a professional to get involved would cost you more in fees than the total balance owed. That's why you should seriously consider paying it and moving on.

If the payment is impossible or you simply can't fathom paying it knowing that the balance showing due is complete B.S., follow these steps:

Step One: Call the number on the notice and ask for an explanation. If you believe the IRS is wrong, ask for a correction and offer to send written proof as a follow-up.

Step Two: Make your entire case again, but this time in writing. Be kind, ask for help, explain why the IRS is wrong, and ask for the adjustment to your taxes to be overturned. You have 60 days to complete this, but do it as soon as possible because the earlier you punt the ball to their side of the field, the better you will feel.

Step Three: If the balance assessed is egregious and something steps one and two won't or can't solve, you can file to go to tax court. Do not try to go on your own, as the IRS will use your inexperience to run circles around you. They have 100+ years of experience collecting taxes and have seen every trick in the book thousands of times. It will probably cost you $10,000 to hire an experienced representative to defend you, so don't go this far unless the tax assessment is big enough to make the representation cost worthwhile.

If you cannot pay the amount due but want to address it, read through the rest of this book to consider the other resolution options available. Remember, there is *ALWAYS* a solution! The good news is that all this back-and-forth correspondence may buy you a few more months before you have to pay anything toward the debt.

What If the IRS Does Not Respond?

This happens a lot and infuriates those simply trying to get an error on their tax account fixed. The people at the IRS love to keep reminding us how busy they are, how understaffed they are, and how sorry they are about not getting back to you. It can take them months to respond.

In the meantime, their computers will keep sending you the collection/ correction letters repeatedly, and interest will continue to be assessed. Answer every one of the letters by sending them copies of your original request for correction/abatement. Do not ignore letters from the IRS; become a thorn in their backside until you get answers.

If you still have no resolution after four months, call the Taxpayer Advocate Service at (877) 777-4778 and ask for assistance. After you have explained that the IRS has not responded to your letters, they may be able to help you get the correction/collection effort cleared up quickly.

One More Consideration That Could Impact Your International Travel Plans

One More Consideration That Could Impact Your International Travel Plans

In 2018, under the Fixing America's Surface Transportation Act, the IRS was granted the right to notify the State Department of taxpayers with "seriously delinquent" tax bills in order to impact their ability to travel internationally. The process is called passport certification and, at present, only happens if your tax debt is over $62,000. The threshold increases slightly each year, but this is where it sat when I wrote this book.

What does this mean? If your tax debt has been certified as "seriously delinquent," the State Department can reject your passport application, deny your passport renewal, or revoke your current passport. To date, the common practice has only been to reject a passport application or renewal, though the right to revoke a current passport is outlined in the Act.

Now, before you begin to worry about the European cruise tickets you just purchased for your vacation later this year, there are actions that can be taken to release the certification. If you enter into an Installment Agreement, are paying towards the debt after negotiating an Offer in Compromise, if an appeal of proposed tax collection is under review, or if collection has been suspended due to a request for Innocent Spouse Relief, the certification will be released. Be aware, however, that it typically takes the State Department 45-60 days to process the release, so don't dawdle!

If you have received the notice advising that your passport has been certified, don't panic, but know it's time to start doing something about the taxes owed. Remember, there's *ALWAYS* a solution!

Summary

Don't dread going to your mailbox every day. If notices from the IRS or state await you when you open the door, fight that impulse to begin quaking in your boots. No matter what the notices say, there is *ALWAYS* a solution. If it's a small bill related to a minor change on your tax return, weigh the costs and benefits to see if you want to fight it or pay it. If it's a larger bill or one of many, open it without fear and send it to your trusted tax debt resolution professional. Remember, allowing them to be proactive on your behalf will keep you in a protected position on the chessboard of dealing with tax debt.

Chapter 6:

What Is the Difference Between a Tax Lien, a Levy, and a Garnishment?

During the tax resolution process, you'll hear some terms bantered about that you will need to understand: tax liens, levies, and garnishments... lions, tigers, and bears, oh my! Each of those terms has a very different meaning and impacts someone with a tax debt differently. Let me give you the basics of each.

Let's Start With "Tax Lien"...

According to the Merriam-Webster Dictionary, a lien is "a charge upon real or personal property for the satisfaction of some debt or duty ordinarily arising by operation of law." In layman's terms, it's the official recording that a debt is owed.

When you purchase a piece of real estate using funds from a loan, the lender will place a lien on the property being purchased to fortify their claim for repayment. They take this legal action to prevent you from being able to sell the property without first paying them back any balance owed on the loan. When you full-pay the loan, the lien is released.

The IRS and state tax agencies operate in the same manner. A tax lien will be filed in the county associated with the last address reported on your income tax return, securing their right to be paid back the taxes owed. Upon paying the debt in one way or another, the lien will be released.

Though the states may have different requirements that must be met before a state tax lien is filed, these are the IRS requirements:

- A tax assessment has been made,
- A demand for payment has been made, and
- The taxpayer has neglected the demand or refused to pay.

Keep in mind that a tax lien doesn't just apply to real estate; it attaches to ALL property or rights of property owned by the taxpayer, including, but not limited to, vehicles, boats, investment accounts, business equipment, etc.

Though this may be uncomfortable to have floating out there on public record, as long as you start addressing the past-due taxes with some type of resolution plan, the IRS or state will not act on the lien to seize assets. In all my years negotiating solutions for my clients, I've never had an IRS or state agent show up at my client's home with a seizure order for their boat sitting in their driveway or their car parked in the garage.

Depending on the type of resolution we identify to address your past-due taxes, we may be able to prevent a tax lien from being filed if one isn't already recorded. Again, being proactive with tax debt is a HUGE part of successfully keeping aggressive collection tactics at bay.

If a tax lien has already been filed, we can sometimes implement a resolution option to seek the lien being withdrawn even before the balance due is paid in full.

The Bite of a Levy

When the IRS or state issues a levy, it is an aggressive action. In plain English, they are saying, "We have told you there is a past-due tax balance owed, you haven't responded to our communications about it, you haven't taken any measures to address it, so we are going to tap the resources we can to recover some or all of the monies owed to us."

ICK!

This is a very real threat to a taxpayer who doesn't start paying attention to the bills received in the mail from the IRS or the state. Eventually, the IRS or state will tire of tapping you on the back to remind you that you owe this money and take matters into their own hands.

When the IRS or state issues a levy order, it starts with a formal notification issued to all banks they know you have accounts with. If you have made any payments to the tax agency in the past, they will see which account those payments have been made from. If you have had any tax refunds directly deposited into a bank account in the past, they will issue levy orders to that bank. If you haven't submitted payments recently and you happen to live in a small town, they'll issue the levy order to all the local banks. If you live in a bigger city, it may take them a bit of time to research the financial records associated with your Social Security Number, but they'll find your bank to issue the order to. They are savvy in their pursuit of repayment!

If a bank levy is issued, first things first: do not panic! Remember, there is *ALWAYS* a solution. With the IRS, once your bank processes a levy order, the funds are not automatically sent to the IRS. Your bank is ordered to withdraw the available funds up to the balance due outlined on the levy order and hold those funds aside for 21 calendar days. These 21 days are given so you have the opportunity to contact the IRS and negotiate a release of the levy order. And yes, before you ask, the IRS *will* order the bank to put the money back into your account if you can work out a solution to the past-due balance owed.

Every state has different rules surrounding how they expect bank levies to be handled. Again, don't panic... but definitely don't sit back and ignore it.

Now, if you are receiving a levy order related to unpaid payroll or income taxes for a business, not only is the business' bank account at risk, but so are your accounts receivable. Typically, the IRS will start trying to get your attention by issuing a levy notice to your bank. But, if a Revenue Officer is assigned to your case and is so inclined, they *can* issue levy orders to all third parties they assume could have outstanding bills or invoices owed to your business.

It's an ugly collection tactic because this hurts not only the income you were counting on to pay things like payroll, utilities, suppliers, etc., but it also hits your reputation, and hits it hard. Suppose one of your customers receives a notice from the IRS or state claiming that $150,000 is owed by your business in unpaid payroll taxes, and any monies they owe you should be sent to the tax agency instead. What is the likelihood they will want to remain one of your customers?

If you receive a final notice that aggressive actions like levies are imminent, TAKE ACTION IMMEDIATELY! Do not call their bluff because you will lose. If you don't know how to address the situation or fear that it's something you aren't equipped to handle, get an experienced tax debt resolution professional involved. The longer you sit on something like this, the more you are putting yourself at risk. There is *ALWAYS* a solution, but it won't happen if you ignore the problem.

Here's an example of why you shouldn't ignore these types of IRS notices:

A new client came to me in a panic: Stephen and his wife owned a restaurant, and the IRS had issued a levy on their bank account just days before payroll. The IRS had confiscated over $22,000 through the levy action; $12,000 of those funds were needed for payroll, and the rest had been earmarked for food and alcohol bills that needed to be addressed. He knew that if he couldn't at least cover the payroll for his kitchen staff and managers, the employees would walk, and he wouldn't be able to keep the business open.

During our initial call, I learned that the business hadn't filed its payroll tax returns for the last two years, and had balances owed for the two years before that amounting to over $120,000,. A Revenue Officer had been reaching out to the business and sending letters, but the client was paralyzed with fear and hadn't responded.

I filed my Power of Attorney the same day and began calling the Revenue Officer. Upon finally connecting with him a few hours later, I heard what I typically do in situations like this, "I have been trying to reach out to your client for four months, and I finally got fed up... that's why the bank levy was issued."

I verified the notices that the Revenue Officer had issued followed the policies and procedures outlined by the Internal Revenue Manual for collection cases like my client's. A Final Notice of Intent to Levy notice had been issued, and the Revenue Officer had waited the appropriate length of time before issuing the bank levy. Knowing that the bank levy action taken was legitimate, I began working with the Revenue Officer about what could be done to release the bank levy.

After two days of bank and forth between the Revenue Officer and my client, we were able to release not only the funds in the bank account needed to cover payroll but were also successful with getting the excess funds released as well. The Revenue Officer made sure we jumped through a lot of hoops before he would release the funds back into the bank account, but we were able to get the money back!

I'm beginning to sound like a broken record, but I want you to remember that there is *ALWAYS* a solution!

How the Tax Agencies Can Take Part of Your Paycheck, A.K.A. "The Garnishment"

If you are in management or have owned a business for a while, you've probably already dealt with a court order to withhold part of an employee's check and forward it to a governing authority. It often happens surrounding child support matters, but it also exists for unpaid tax bills.

Now, a garnishment does not happen just out of the blue. Several notices about a tax debt are issued, with the last being a clear warning shot across the bow: "If you don't address this immediately, we will take aggressive collection actions." These actions typically start with bank levies, but especially with the states, it will be in the form of wage garnishments if you are a W-2 employee.

If the IRS takes this action, the amount that can be taken each paycheck is limited based upon the amount of your wages, how often you are paid in a month, and how many dependents you have. This typically calculates to about 25-50% of your income. As with all things in the tax world, each state has its own rules surrounding garnishments and if there is a limit to how much they can take.

For most Americans, a wage garnishment will cause a serious cramp to their financial condition. It will affect bills you have set for auto-draft, your ability to buy groceries, and ultimately throw your entire monthly budget on its ear.

If you have any way to take action today to prevent a garnishment from going into effect, you want to do so immediately. Get an experienced tax debt resolution professional involved to help, but make sure they have handled this type of sensitive situation before. You don't want someone cutting their teeth using your case as their testing ground!

Summary

Knowledge is power. Knowing the difference between a tax lien, a levy, and a garnishment and what each means to you is essential if you have a tax debt. Ideally, you want to take action to prevent any of them from coming into play. However, know that if you are reading this after one or all of these actions have been taken, there is *ALWAYS* a solution. The wise thing to do is to get your cards face up on the table as quickly as possible with someone who will be on your side. Come up with a plan to negotiate the amount or the payment schedule and then stick to the plan. You'll get this horrible situation behind you and enjoy a peace of mind that you probably have not felt for a long time.

Chapter 7:

Can I Change My Name or Move to Brazil? Can I Challenge the Law?

I know that having a tax debt can lead to many sleepless nights. And when you're lying there, staring at the ceiling, your mind can wander down some strange paths. This is when some of the far-fetched "maybe" solutions pop into your head.

The three most common "what if I…" thoughts often shared with me are:

1. Can I go to Mexico, get a fake ID, return to America as an immigrant, and start over under a new name?

2. What are my chances of leaving the country and never returning? Can I be a tax fugitive in Brazil?

3. Can we countersue the IRS? I heard that Congress did not actually ratify the 16th Amendment, so they can't legally ask me to pay, right?

Let's look at the reality of these ideas.

Can You Leave for Mexico and Then Come Back?

This may have been possible 25 years ago, but not anymore. Homeland Security has made it a lot tougher than you think. You will not blend in when you go to Mexico, and with all the cartel issues, it's probably not someplace you want to be if you aren't snuggled safely inside a resort compound.

If you do happen to get your hands on some fake IDs and make it back to the US border, the odds of them passing scrutiny are slim. Homeland Security will probably interview and fingerprint you, revealing that the ID you tried to use was fake. With this happening, you will end up with more legal issues than if you had just dealt with the tax problems to begin with.

If the stars align in your favor and you somehow manage to get past the U.S. Border Patrol and Homeland Security, the only work you'll ever be able to get is hard labor for cash under the table. Because you won't pass the identification process to secure an ITIN (what immigrants use instead of a Social Security Number), you won't be able to gain employment as a W-2 employee.

In a nutshell, this isn't a viable option.

Can I Slip Out of the Country and Become a Fugitive?

Now, this is a concept that could genuinely seem attractive: leave the U.S. and move to a foreign country.

However, think about the things you would be forgoing: all the Social Security benefits you have built up during your career (yes, we will still have those benefits as long as the United States or something close to it is in place when you hit your later years), family history, the freedoms granted by our Constitution, etc. And think about the people with WAY more money and resources than you who have tried to do this but failed.

John McAfee, the inventor of the McAfee Antivirus program, was accused of tax evasion by the United States Government. In 2019, he jumped ship and headed to Belize to avoid ongoing persecution for not having paid taxes for over eight years and other pending investigations into financial affairs. He was arrested in Spain on behalf of the US Department of Justice for tax evasion and a fraudulent crypto scheme.

While waiting for extradition back to the US, he ended up dying in his prison cell in Barcelona. This is an extreme story, I know, but it proves that even someone with the money and power wielded by a wealthy inventor and former presidential candidate couldn't find a way to avoid the long arm of the US Government.

The truth is, everyone who has tried to become a fugitive has ended up 'ratted out' by someone and got captured, or they ended up dead by mysterious circumstances. Plus, there are only 21 countries that do not have an extradition treaty with the USA. The list includes countries like Vietnam, Belarus, Botswana, Iran, and Somalia. Do you really want to move there just so you don't have to pay taxes?

Can I Sue the IRS Because the Amendment Was Not Ratified?

NO… and don't let any slick salesman try to convince you otherwise. In 1913, the 16th Amendment was ratified and recognized as the law of the land, granting Congress *the power to lay and collect taxes on incomes, from whatever source derived, without apportionment among the several States and without regard to any census or enumeration.* The income tax is legal no matter what you think or what you may have heard from some salesman over the phone during a call that started with, "So, I understand you have a tax lien filed against you." The IRS has never lost a case questioning the legality of the tax law. Don't waste your time, effort, or money chasing this notion.

Can I Walk Away and Ignore the Entire Collection Process?

Yes, if you file your returns. Remember that not paying your taxes won't cause you to go to prison in 99.9% of the cases, but not filing your returns will. Also, lying to the IRS about your income or assets could land you in jail because of the "penalty of perjury" statement on every financial form you must submit when under the scrutiny of the Collections Department.

If you want to ignore every letter and collection effort they throw at you, technically, you can. However, be very clear about what they can do through their attempts to collect the debt: seizing the funds in your bank account, seizing your retirement and investment accounts, garnishing your pay, and seizing your real estate. The IRS has ten years to collect on each tax balance accrued from the date it hits the official record on your tax account. Though every state is different, ten years is their average collection timeframe, though some can extend to the lifetime the tax account is valid (meaning until you pass away). That's a llloooonnnngggg timeframe to commit to dealing with them, especially since the debt will continue to snowball with assessed penalties and interest.

One Last Story About Trying To Be Sneaky About Your Financial Situation

When the IRS asks you about an asset or income stream, they almost always know the answer beforehand; if not, they can dig in far beyond what you would think to find the answers they seek. Depending on how the negotiations are going, they *can* try to trick you into lying to them. If you don't feel comfortable talking to the collection agent, hire me or some other experienced tax debt resolution professional; that's why we have the licenses to represent you before the tax agencies. We are damn good at not just dealing with them, but we can help you understand what is happening, why, and how we are going to get you past it. Plus, we won't accidentally blurt out something that will come back to haunt you.

In Oregon, about 15 years ago, an elderly couple failed to report the sale of some high-value art that had been in the family for generations. The couple got audited, and the funds were found and recorded as unreported income to the tune of over $180,000. The couple was angry about the IRS trying to get a piece of the sale. They needed the money to live on and thought it was unfair that they would be asked to pay capital gains tax on something that had been in the family for generations. As a result, they ignored the notices sent by the IRS asking for the tax to be addressed.

A Revenue Officer was assigned to the case. After many unsuccessful attempts to communicate with them via phone calls and letters, he sent bank record summons to their bank and issued an official summons for them to appear for a financial disclosure interview. During the interview, the Revenue Officer compiled the official IRS financial statement (Form 433-A, Collection Information Statement for Wage Earners and Self-Employed Individuals) and had the couple sign the document under penalty of perjury at the end of the meeting. A week later, the couple was notified that federal perjury charges were brought against them.

You see, when the Revenue Officer summonsed the bank records, he found wires made by the couple to a bank. Upon investigating the information further, he found it was located in the Caribbean, and the couple did not disclose the bank account on the financial statement they signed during the interview. Whether it was simply an oversight by the couple or whether they intentionally didn't disclose it because it was offshore and they thought the IRS wouldn't find it, it doesn't matter. As a result of the charges, a 75-year-old husband and 73-year-old wife each ended up spending 18 months in Federal prison.

Did the situation truly warrant Federal perjury charges? Maybe. However, given the couple's unwillingness to speak with the IRS and work out a solution, then "forgetting" to list the Caribbean bank account as an asset, the IRS had sufficient justification to pursue those charges. This is why, even if you think you can figure out how to work with the IRS or state to address a tax debt, it may be beneficial to have a professional in your corner. Someone who can look out for your best interests as the game of solving a tax debt plays out.

Summary

It may sound sexy to pack a bag, grab some stacks of cash and a fake passport out of the safe hidden in the back of your closet, and blow up your home as you drive down the street to catch a plane headed overseas. But it's unrealistic, which is why we never hear about similar stories in the news. It's not a real scenario that plays out. It's fiction, and it will not go well for you.

It is far easier to suck it up and deal with the tax debt; it may take a few years, and it may be a bit painful to limit your other desires as you knuckle down and deal with the tax debt. But, in the end, you'll come out the other side and won't have to worry anymore about it. You'll be able to refocus on building your financial future. Remember, there's *ALWAYS* a solution… doing something drastic like these ideas just isn't worth it.

Chapter 8:

The Ten Best Strategies to Deal with an IRS or State Tax Debt

Our first and biggest goal is to keep any problems from getting to the point where the IRS or state is filing tax liens, draining your bank accounts, or seizing your assets. Now, if you are reading this after collection actions have started, let's move quickly to put the brakes on the collection efforts and try to devise a plan that keeps your life intact.

This book is filled with many stories about people just like you with tax troubles. Every situation is different, and every resolution is tailored to the taxpayer's unique financial condition and total tax debt(s owed. The important thing is not to delay because you want to maintain as much control over the outcome as possible. Remember, there is *ALWAYS* a solution...

These are the most common and legitimate ways to address a tax debt:

NOTE: You are NOT in control of the outcome if you do not open those letters and take charge of the situation.

---

1. Replace Substitute Returns Filed by the IRS or State

Whenever a tax return is filed on a taxpayer's behalf by the IRS or state because they never received the return, they *always* file it in a manner that taxes your reported income at the highest tax level possible with no regard for credits or deductions. Meet with a tax return preparation professional to review the reported income and the balance deemed owed when the IRS or state compiled the return and assess replacing the estimated tax balance with an accurate return.

2. Leveraging Real Estate

In some instances, it is easier to tap the equity in real estate you own to address a past-due tax debt than to succumb to lengthy repayment plans that continue to accrue penalties and interest. If there isn't a tax lien already recorded by the IRS or state and this option is attractive to you, act fast! Get it done before a lien is filed. Once one is on record, some extra hoops have to be jumped through.

3. Audit Challenge

Did you know that a taxpayer can ask the IRS or state to reconsider the results even after an audit is conducted and a determination is made? Usually, this resolution option can be considered when the taxpayer either wasn't aware of the pending audit due to an address change or couldn't provide sufficient documentation for consideration before the deadline to respond expired.

4. Currently Not-Collectible

The IRS and most states have this program available when a taxpayer cannot address the past due taxes owed while tending to their ongoing tax obligations and basic needs for health and welfare. This sounds ideal, but the way the IRS and states analyze a taxpayer's financial condition to determine what is "necessary" is very different than most taxpayer's assessments of their own financial condition.

5. Installment Agreement

Setting up an Installment Agreement to address a past-due tax debt is one of the most common forms of resolution, no matter whether the tax agency owed is the IRS or the state. This type of arrangement lets you address the debt with monthly installments over an agreed-upon duration of time.

6. Offer In Compromise

An Offer in Compromise, also known as an Offer in Settlement by some states, is a legal way to settle a past-due tax debt owed. The negotiated settlement is typically based on the taxpayer's equity in assets and ongoing income versus "allowable" expenses.

7. Penalty Abatement

A Penalty Abatement request allows the taxpayer to point the finger for the accrual of the tax debt at a specific incident or cause that was outside of the taxpayer's control. This is an avenue to request the lowering of the total tax bill that needs to be paid back when other options aren't applicable.

8. Bankruptcy

While most people buck the notion, filing for bankruptcy can sometimes be the most appropriate opyion based on the type of tax owed, the taxpayer's financial condition, and other debts that may be owed.

9. Innocent or Injured Spouse Relief

These resolution options come into play when a tax debt is assessed against a couple that has filed a joint income tax return related to one spouse's financial activities or when there is collection of tax payment from a spouse that did not have any responsibility for a past-due tax debt.

10. Expiration of Collection Statutes

Once a tax bill is officially recorded, the IRS and most states have a limited timeframe they can collect on the debt. Sometimes, we can make strategic moves on a taxpayer's account that allow those collection timeframes to expire without collecting payments to be applied to the debt.

In the following chapters, I will go into more detail about some of these resolution options and how we employ them to address a past-due IRS or state tax debt. As I have already told you many times in this book and will continue to repeat many times in the coming pages, there is *ALWAYS* a solution to a tax debt... we just need to find the solution that best fits your unique situation.

Chapter 9:

Addressing Missing Tax Returns or Fixing an Over-Estimated Substitute for Return

If this is your situation, don't panic; you are not alone. The IRS estimates that over 10 Million people do not file their income tax returns each year, which equates to approximately 5% of the taxpayers required to file. For some reason, we get behind the eight ball and the burden of filing the annual tax return becomes overwhelming. So, we skip this year.

That turns out to be fairly painless; it takes the tax agencies a minimum of a year to realize you haven't filed. That leads to often skipping next year as well because we don't want anyone to notice last year's missing return. This becomes a cascading series of choices that eventually come back to haunt you.

You will have to file eventually, or the IRS and state will file a return for you, and you will NOT like what they say you owe. And to add salt to the already-open wound, penalties and interest will be assessed on the estimated tax balance going back to the original due date the return was to be filed.

But remember, there is *ALWAYS* a solution if you actively pursue one. The emotional pain of worrying about what the IRS or state will eventually do is greater than the pain of getting caught up.

File and Fight When You Are Down on Your Luck

When I ask clients why they did not file for 3 or 4 years, they tell me about financial problems and how they were close to broke. A common reply is, "I was waiting until I got back on my feet so that I could clear it all up at once."

The best time to address a past-due tax situation is now. If you want to negotiate a settlement with the IRS or state, remember that it will be based on your current financial condition. If you wait until you have $50,000 in the bank, they will want that money to be applied toward the tax debt owed. If you have $500 in the bank, the IRS or state will be more willing to settle your case with an Offer in Compromise, officially recognize your inability to pay and place the debt into Currently Not-Collectible, or agree to low-dollar installments quickly. The nightmare will be over.

Other Reasons to Get Your Returns Filed Immediately

- You will lose your refund and tax credits - If you have a refund coming and fail to file, you will lose that refund after three years. You might also lose the earned income tax credit (or the other tax credits you may be eligible for) if you are four years late.

- You can't borrow money or get a mortgage - If you don't have current tax returns, your opportunities for expanding your business or buying a home are significantly reduced because you won't qualify for credit or loans.

- Your name will pop up to the top of the computer screen sooner or later - Since the creation of the Homeland Security Act after 9/11, the amount of tracking our government does of its citizens has gone through the roof. They already know 95% of what goes on in the economy, which means they know if you have a job, they know almost every purchase you have made, and they know about most things you own.

66

You won't hear much from the IRS or state about a missing tax return initially, but eventually, they figure it out. Somewhere between 12 and maybe even as long as 72 months, the IRS or state will start sending you letters. Please do not ignore them. It just makes everything worse.

SFRs and the Danger That Comes with Them

If you did not file for the past one or more years, given the IRS and state's jaded viewpoints, they figure you owe them money. But by law, they cannot initiate tax collection efforts without a debt determined. So, if they have sent letters asking for the missing tax return(s) and you do not respond, they will file an estimated tax return for you, known as the SFR (Substitute for Return).

You are not going to like the returns they file. They will estimate how much you make based on other information sources like payroll reports, bank statements, the real estate property you own, eBay or Venmo numbers, and hundreds of other sources.

They will guess your income based on your home, car, bank balance, and other assets and can even look at your social media to see if you have been bragging about all the places you have traveled to or the luxury car in your garage. When they file your return for you, they will round up.

They will give you your standard deductions but ignore everything else, like mortgage interest deductions. Your tax bill at the end of their calculation could cause a four-star general to sweat bullets.

This happened to a colleague's client who owned a vacation house in California a while back. In 1999, he paid $2,000,000 for a home on the beach, and his family went there a few times a year. Except for a house sitter (to prevent squatters), the house was vacant the rest of the year. They did not put it on Airbnb because that online marketplace did not exist in 2007 when these events played out.

The forty-nine weeks a year the family was not in California, they did not earn any income on the property; it was strictly a vacation home. Seven years after they bought the house, the state decided the client should pay California income tax because they owned real property in California.

The client refused to file; he told the collection agent from the Franchise Tax Board, "I do not have an income in California; I'm not a resident. You have no track record of a bank account or a paycheck for me in this state. All I have is a vacation house, and by the way, I already pay $15,000 a year in property taxes."

The collection agent replied something along the lines of, "Well, if you don't like our tax laws, maybe you shouldn't own property in California," which escalated the undercurrent feelings of the situation.

The tax collector was used to people cowering when he called, but he severely underestimated this taxpayer's resolve. With the conclusion of this heated exchange, the collection agent became more aggressive and filed a $36,000 tax lien for 2007 income tax. Without further warning, he made an estimated income tax assessment and filed the lien.

The client was unaware of the tax lien until it was disclosed to him during a business loan application process because the notices had been mailed to the California property; the loan was denied solely because of the erroneous tax lien. At this point, my colleague was retained by the irate taxpayer.

The client hired my colleague because he was so upset over the whole affair that he knew he'd be too agitated and unable to keep his cool as he sought a reasonable solution to the erroneous assessment. (Remember that when you are angry, you say things that do not help your case; that's another reason to consider using a tax debt resolution professional… we can take the emotions out of the situation on your behalf!)

When my colleague asked the Franchise Tax Board agent how they came up with the $36,000 number, he was told, "In California, if you own a $2,000,000 home, you must make at least $400,000 - so the state tax on that amount of income is around $36,000." That's a pretty slick answer, but one that is full of fault! My colleague was told that if the state was to release the lien, a state income tax return had to be filed, proving that the estimated income tax bill was erroneous.

Everything worked out in the end. My colleague and the taxpayer had a correct income tax return compiled reflecting the accurate "zero" income earned in California, and eventually, the Franchise Tax Board released the tax lien.

We can learn from this tale: if a tax agency wants to see a return, it is best to get it done, or the situation can careen out of control. Even if the tax return shows you owe taxes and you don't have the means to pay it, it will be easier to work out the problem if you don't hold back on filing the returns.

How to Handle an SFR Situation

You'll be notified that the IRS or state has filed missing returns on your behalf and that you have 30 days to file the correct ones based on your own numbers. If they don't receive a tax return from you correcting the proposed tax bill, you will typically have another 60 days before they start collection efforts.

At this point, you really need to start taking action. The best move is to get a tax professional involved to compile the missing tax return(s). If you are unable to locate all of your records, you can at least start by asking for the wage and income transcripts from the IRS or state.

Ignoring the IRS at this point is how people end up having to address grossly exaggerated tax bills that can end up costing them their bank accounts, investments, and plans for the foreseeable future.

Report Everything

When a friend of mine filed for bankruptcy three years ago, the lawyer gave her some solid advice. "I want you to throw everything on your list of debts and liabilities. If you borrowed $1,000 from your cousin five years ago, put it on the list." The idea was that once this event is over, we don't want someone returning and making it hard for you again.

The same advice applies to your tax returns: if you have an outstanding tax return that needs to be filed years later, the IRS and state will question everything reported. They don't trust you at this point. From experience, they know that someone who has not filed for a few years is most likely to underreport income or exaggerate deductions. It is best to take the time to ensure every penny of income received is reported and that the expenses or deductions claimed can be proven without a shadow of a doubt. Again, you don't want any future surprises.

With the plans to address the tax debt with a resolution, you want to make sure you only go through the process once. You don't want to file the tax returns, go through the steps of negotiating a resolution, and then have to do it all over again in a year or two because an audit of the return revealed unreported income or disqualified something claimed.

What If the IRS or State Hasn't Caught on Yet About My Missing Returns?

First of all, please recognize that they do know... they just haven't gotten around to you yet. Most people who come to me with tax account concerns over missing tax returns just found out they could not buy a home, get a security clearance, secure bonding on a big construction job, or some other business opportunity because they have outstanding tax returns.

If you need to provide copies of your past tax returns for any personal or business reason, you cannot create returns and then give them to the bank or any other third party without turning them in to the IRS and state at the same time.

If the lending institution asks for copies of your past tax returns, they will verify them with the tax agencies. That means they will ask the IRS to confirm that the return was filed and that no balance is owed. Your loan will be disallowed if the returns are not on file at the IRS. Believe me; you're happy to get turned down in this situation. That action constitutes fraud on a federal level; this is one action that is severe enough to land you in prison.

If you owe taxes on the unfiled returns, you can include a check to address the tax due, or you can send them in without payment and start negotiating a resolution plan.

Keep Your Record Clean

We want to keep the IRS or state from filing a tax lien, if possible. Even once it's been satisfied, it can stay on your credit report for up to 10 years. By law, tax liens cannot affect your consumer credit *score*, but they will count against you when seeking a high-dollar loan, such as a mortgage on a home.

There's *ALWAYS* a Solution

You've heard me say this repeatedly in this book, and I will continue to say it. Every client I've ever gotten over a tax debt hurdle has come out the other side feeling better than when they first came to me. Even if you can't pay your taxes, have not filed for years, or have liens… do not think your life is over. If you are focused on securing a solution to the tax debt problem and take steps toward it, you will get to the other side.

Summary

In most cases, you will not go to prison because you can't pay your taxes. Failing to file or filing returns with false information gets people in legal trouble. The first choice of the IRS is to get the return, not ask for a prison sentence. Catching up on unfiled returns may be uncomfortable, but it will be much less painful than waking up at 3 a.m. thinking about all the bad things that might happen to your family if the IRS or state brings down the hammer.

Chapter 10:

Perhaps Leveraging Your Real Estate Holdings Is an Answer

I'm sure your hackles got a bit raised when you read the title of this chapter. I'm not suggesting that tapping the hard-earned equity in your real estate is always going to be the best way to address a tax debt with the IRS or state, but it could be the most beneficial way to have your money work for you in a smarter way. Please stick with me for a bit here…

Anthony reached out to me about a tax debt issue he had with the IRS. He lived in Missouri with his wife and kids and made decent money as a beer distributor. But, he had a tax bill from the IRS of $85,000 that was causing him and his wife to sweat because the collection notices were threatening seizure.

After walking through their financial situation, I found they had no other substantial debts besides this dang IRS bill. We talked about their investments, which were in the six-figure range. No way would we tap that asset unless somebody's life was on the line. Since that wasn't their situation, we moved on. As we were talking further, their residence caught my attention. As it turns out, they had lived in their home for fifteen years, and it was almost paid off.

Knowing that the IRS was charging 7% interest at the time on unpaid income tax debts, and any interest paid on a tax bill is not tax-deductible, I started introducing the idea of refinancing the home to secure sufficient money to pay off the tax bill. (I know, I know… nobody wants to tap their equity if they don't need to… keep sticking with me!)

Remember that the interest you pay on a mortgage on your primary residence is tax-deductible. They would be ahead even if the loan they secured was at a 6.5% interest rate! This is why considering all options available to you to leverage your money is one of the smartest things you can do when considering a tax debt situation.

Anthony was able to secure a loan at 5.75% to pay the tax debt off in full, the tax lien was released, and the family was able to claim the interest paid on the note on their annual income tax return as a deduction.

> **NOTE:** The IRS and states use tax liens as a bargaining chip. Make it work for you in the best way possible, given your financial condition and the options available.

One Caution to Heed: the Tax Lien

If the IRS or state has filed a tax lien against you related to past-due taxes, the lien has to be addressed if you plan to do anything with real estate to address the taxes owed. As discussed in Chapter 6, the tax lien is the IRS or state's way of legally ensuring their rights to collect against your assets for application to the past due taxes owed.

There Are a Few Ways That Tax Debts and Liens Can Be Addressed By Selling Real Estate:

1. Sell the asset and pay the tax debt in full – when doing this, the title company handling the sale will secure a lien payoff confirmation from the IRS or state, and the tax bill will be paid directly by the title company at closing. As long as you have sufficient proceeds from the sale at closing, this is a relatively straightforward process to go through.

2. If you are selling an asset but can only pay a chunk of money towards the tax debt – The IRS and state would much rather get a chunk of money towards the tax debt versus nothing at all. It just takes some extra time and involves petitioning the lien department at the IRS or state to remove the lien on the asset at closing in exchange for receiving the funds available from the sale.

3. Sell a piece of real estate that is fully encumbered – even if the IRS or state won't get a dime from the sale, they will still consider releasing the tax lien secured against the asset. Here's why: if you can explain to the IRS or state that with the sale of the property, you will have $1,000 extra each month to start giving them through an Installment Agreement, why wouldn't they agree???

I want to give you a word of caution about this: make sure your Realtor understands that a tax lien is involved with the sale when you sign your listing contract with them. It takes time for the lien department to consider any lien release without receiving payment for the entire tax debt. Your Realtor must manage the buyer's timeline expectations to get everything handled before closing.

Here's an Example of Why You Should Follow My Direction

Manuel and Rosita were clients of mine in Texas who had a $190,000 income tax bill with the IRS. They were in their 60s, and while they loved their home, it was too big for them now that their kids were grown and had families. The resolution strategy we discussed was to sell the house and apply all the money available toward the tax debt. The home's value had decreased to $385,000, and they still had a mortgage owed of $250,000 from a re-fi they had done eight years prior. Once that step was taken, we would then set up an Installment Agreement to address the balance remaining due.

We laid the game plan out: get the property listed; when they received an acceptable contract, I would submit the paperwork to the lien department asking for a discharge of the tax lien in exchange for the roughly $100,000 available to be applied to the tax bill. I cautioned Manuel and Rosita multiple times in multiple conversations to tell their Realtor about the tax lien and the roughly 4-6 weeks I would need to handle the lien for the sale. I asked to be placed in touch with the Realtor so I could walk her through the process. "Okay, no problem..." was the reply I continued to receive, but I never heard from the Realtor.

Two weeks later, Rosita called me with the good news that they received a contract for the full asking price. The buyer was very excited about the home and wanted to push for closing within three weeks. Woah, there! I jogged Rosita's memory about our multiple conversations that outlined the process for handling the tax lien. "Is there something we can do? Manuel and I haven't told our Realtor about the tax lien."

I initiated a conference call with the Realtor, Manuel, and Rosita, and disclosed the tax lien hiccup to her. She was not happy at all! I went to work with the submission of a tax lien discharge petition, asking for expedited handling. It took multiple phone calls to the lien department, asking for managers over and over until I got someone who grabbed the case and started working with us. It took over 18 hours of my and my staff's time to secure cooperation from the IRS, but we finally got the IRS to agree to remove the tax lien in exchange for the sale proceeds two days before closing.

My advice from this tale is pretty simple: don't expect a miracle to happen like this one! If you have an experienced tax debt resolution professional involved, they may be able to secure a similar outcome, but it takes a LOT of muscle and persistence. It's much better to plan accordingly and keep your realtor fully apprised of the entire situation. Have your tax debt resolution professional walk him/her through the process so they know what to expect and can appropriately manage the buyer's expectations.

When I asked Manuel and Rosita at the end of their escapade why they didn't tell their Realtor about the tax lien and get her in contact with me, they said they were simply embarrassed about the entire tax debt and didn't want her to think less of them. I can completely understand that rationale and thought process. However, it could have been an absolute disaster if they didn't have an experienced person like me who has gone through the tax lien discharge process hundreds of times before. There is no way the sale would have closed on time, and they may have lost the buyer's interest. There is *ALWAYS* a solution, but to get the best outcome, make sure all parties that need to know about the tax debt have the whole story.

What About Securing a Loan Against Your Property?

If you have equity in your home that you would like to tap to address the tax debt, sometimes a loan is a great option. Remember, the penalties and interest you pay on a tax debt are not tax-deductible, and they keep snowballing. Sometimes it *is* a smart decision to suck it up and pull some of the equity. It will undoubtedly be a smarter way to leverage your resources. I would much rather you pay 6.0% interest on a loan that is tax deductible than paying a debt with long-term payments that accrue 8-10% between penalties and interest for the next few years!

There Are Two Ways That Tax Debts and Liens Can Be Addressed with Lending:

1. Secure a loan against your real estate to pay the tax debt in full - this is the more straightforward process. Your lender may raise an eyebrow over the tax lien and will definitely disclose to you that the tax lien will cost you an extra point or two of interest, but most will approve the loan if the tax debt is your only financial indiscretion.

2. Secure a loan against your real estate to pay a portion of the tax debt or nothing at all – wait, what??? Yes, if it makes sense, you can petition the IRS or state to move their tax lien behind a lender if they will get some cash out of the transaction or if doing so will put you in a position to start paying them a monthly payment.

I will tell you that most lenders don't even know about option 2. They aren't taught that the IRS and most states will "subordinate" their tax lien position if it makes sense to do so. However, I am here to tell you that it can be done. Your job would be to find a lender who will give you a loan as long as the IRS or state will take a junior position to them… you find that, and we can get this done!

I'm going back a fair bit with this tale, but the principle is relevant: Jerry was a Vietnam Veteran with a small taxi business he and his wife, Susanne, managed in South Carolina. They didn't make much money, but between the small profits realized and his disability check from the government, they made ends meet. Jerry and Susanne had a tax debt related to their self-employment income tax of $180,000 for tax years 2010, 2011, 2012, 2013, 2014, 2015, 2016, and 2017. Due to their poor credit history, they had been locked into a high-interest rate loan for their home when they purchased it in 2004.

Upon reviewing their financial situation, I introduced the idea of refinancing their property to at least alleviate some of the monthly payment pressure Jerry and Susanne had been dealing with. Home values in their area had decreased, so the property they had purchased for $280,000 was down to $225,000, and the loan still had a balance of about $210,000. The IRS was getting cranky over the unpaid tax bill, threatening to take levy actions against their personal and business bank accounts, so we needed to do something quickly. Jerry didn't think a lender would touch them with the tax lien on the property, but I convinced him to try with a focus on Veteran-friendly lenders. Lo and behold, within a week, Jerry had found a lender who would provide a loan to them at 5.9% if we could do something about the IRS tax lien.

I pulled together a subordination request outlining that though the IRS wouldn't get a dime from the refinance, it would drop their monthly mortgage payment to a more reasonable amount. That move would free up $480.00 per month that Jerry and Susanne could dedicate towards a monthly payment on the tax debt. It wouldn't be a significant payment, but it would be better than the nothing they had previously been able to afford! And guess what? The IRS agreed. We got the IRS to subordinate its lien position, the loan approved, and the Installment Agreement set up within a matter of three months.

Summary

Remember, there is *ALWAYS* a solution. The IRS and states, more than anything else, want to start minimizing the amount you owe them. Sometimes, it takes a bit of creativity and pushing past perceived roadblocks to get it done… but where there's a will, there's a way.

Chapter 11:

What Is CNC and How Do I Qualify?

CNC stands for "Currently Not-Collectible." It's exactly as it sounds: the tax agency recognizes you don't have the financial means to address the past-due taxes owed. While this is the official designation with the IRS, most states have a similar collection status if they don't call it by the same monicker.

I had a client, Donald, who was in his late 60s, living in New Mexico and making his living in commercial real estate. He had two single-member LLCs, one focusing on commercial real estate transactions, and the other was for a mentoring program he ran, teaching newbies the ins and outs of success in the industry. Donald had a tax debt going back over twelve years, with the oldest being from substitute returns he never refuted.

After working with him for a year to bring him into compliance with his ongoing estimated income tax payment obligations for the current income he was earning, his health took a turn for the worse. Due to a severe back injury, he was rendered unable to sit comfortably, was only able to stand for fifteen minutes at a time, and spent most of his time flat on his back in bed. As such, his income entered a drastic tailspin.

The IRS was hounding us to begin addressing the past-due taxes, which amounted to over $420,000. Armed with financial statements reflecting his dire financial condition and a letter from the surgeon planning to operate on Donald, I negotiated the IRS placing the case into a CNC status. By negotiating this, we got the IRS to back off; he was allowed time to go through the surgery and recovery and begin slowly building back his self-employed income without fear of nasty collection tactics from the IRS, such as bank account levies.

How Can I Qualify?

To qualify for CNC, you must be operating pretty much at "net zero" each month and have minimal to no equity in assets.

The IRS or state will ask you to pull together a financial disclosure statement outlining everything you own, how much it's worth, your income, and an outline of your monthly expenses. They will whittle down the expenses to what is deemed "allowable," double-check the values you claimed for your assets, and determine if you have anything left over at the end of the month to pay towards the debt. If they come up with "zero," they will deem you "uncollectible."

Now, if you have equity in a vehicle you use to commute to work every day, that isn't enough to disqualify you from a CNC status. On the other hand, if you have $100,000 equity in your residence, they may put you through some hoops with a request to apply for a loan to see if you can pay the tax debt from the proceeds.

> **NOTE:** If the IRS or state is trying to force you to tap equity in real estate to address a tax debt but you wouldn't be able to make the monthly payments associated with that type of loan, PUSH BACK!!!

How Long Can I Stay in a CNC Status?

Keep in mind that the CNC designation is not an everlasting answer to a tax debt. Though the states have different rules and policies for their programs, they typically follow the IRS' path, which is to have the account placed into CNC for a timeframe of two years or until an income change is noticed on the wage and income disclosure documents that pass through the government each year. If you win the lottery six months after your tax account is placed into CNC status, they are going to come knocking at your door for payment of the taxes owed.

When an account is placed in CNC, you agree to grant the IRS and state the right to occasionally ask for an updated financial statement. They have this practice in place to see if anything may have changed with your financial condition, thereby allowing them to start expecting payment towards the past-due taxes owed.

I have placed client accounts into CNC, and because nothing changed with their income level, two years later, they got a letter from the IRS asking for a new financial statement to be submitted. I have had client accounts placed into CNC, and because nothing changed with their income level and the computer system at the IRS didn't flag their account for follow-up, they never heard from the IRS again about the debt other than annual reminder letters about the balance owed. You never know which end of the spectrum you will fall on, so don't count on never hearing from them again. Just know that this option gives you more breathing room if you need it and can qualify for it.

The Pros and Cons of a CNC Status

A big pro to the CNC option is that the collection statutes (the timeframe the tax agency is allowed to collect on each debt) continue to run. So, for example, if your tax debt had six years left for the IRS to collect on it when you enter a CNC status, that timeframe will continue to whittle down without you having to make payments towards the debt.

While CNC may seem like an excellent solution for you, keep in mind (as with all things with the tax agencies) that a big "con" asterisk comes along with this type of designation: penalties and interest will continue to accrue on the debt until it is either paid or until the time allowed to collect on the debt expires.

If you think your financial condition will change for the better in the future and within the timeframe that the IRS or state will still have to collect on the debt, be careful. At the time of writing this book, the IRS is charging 8.0% interest per annum on unpaid tax balances compounded daily. Most states follow suit, with some being a percentage point lower and some a tad higher. It doesn't matter which tax agency you have the debt with; interest will continue to accrue. Penalties will continue to be charged on the tax balances until they hit the maximum thresholds, which vary.

Let's say, for example, you have a tax debt in 2024 of $50,000 owed to the IRS, and it is placed into CNC. A year later, you get a different job with a significant pay increase. You don't alert the IRS to your new-found ability to begin making payments towards the debt, hoping to continue flying under the radar so you can catch up on other bills. In 2026, the IRS catches up with you, and the debt has increased to $58,675 simply because of the interest that continued to accrue.

Summary

As with all things concerning tax debt and the tax agencies, be careful with how you address the debt. Something may look good at the onset, but may be worse for you in the long run. This is why having an experienced tax debt resolution professional on your side who knows these programs inside and out is one of the smartest things you can do for yourself. Having a tax debt is stressful and tricky to deal with. You wouldn't go to a general physician for brain surgery! The same principle applies to dealing with a tax debt... an expert will net you the best outcome possible.

Chapter 12:

One of the Most Common Options: Setting Up a Payment Plan

It has always been known that if you have a tax debt, you can set up monthly payment agreements to address it. In the past, however, the rules for these programs were tight. You had to pay the debt within a stipulated timeframe, whether you could afford the monthly payments or not. Now? Not so much.

The "kinder, gentler" IRS that was ushered in with the reformation acts in the late 90s gave some breathing room to the taxpayer with consideration granted to the taxpayer's necessary health and welfare expenses, and the states followed suit. In 2011, the IRS went even further by enacting the "Fresh Start Program."

If you believe the hard-pressing sales tactics of many of the tax resolution mills, "the Fresh Start Program is a limited-time only offer that had better be jumped on right away by every taxpayer with a debt because it will end soon." All that's missing from those ads is a "But wait! There's more!!!" added in. I'm here to tell you that that's simply not the case!

Like all other resolution programs established by the IRS, the Fresh Start Program will stay in place until new laws are passed. As of the writing of this book, there is no pending legislation to revoke the extra allowances granted by that program, so don't fall for any of the "limited time only" garbage the salespeople are trying to throw your way.

The Fresh Start Program expanded the Installment Agreement options and touched on other resolution strategies, including the Offer in

Compromise program, penalty abatements, and lien procedures. It was more of a marketing ploy by the IRS to entice taxpayers with past-due taxes to address their accounts. It was a program designed to make you feel good about catching up on your taxes above anything else, a way to think you have drawn a line in the sand and are starting fresh.

NOTE: If we can get to the IRS before they file a Notice of Federal Tax Lien, we may be able to use one of the Installment Agreement programs to prevent one from being filed! Your financial rebound will be easier if nobody can find a public record of your tax debts.

The Main Installment Agreement Options Offered by the IRS

As with most things with the IRS, they have focused on standardizing the resolution program options available to address past-due tax debts, including the various Installment Agreement options they will consider. Not only does this take away the human element of favoring one taxpayer over another, but it also prevents someone on the phone lines from punishing a taxpayer who may be a bit "heated" when they call in.

Here are the main standardized options available at the time that I was writing this book:

- Guaranteed Installment Agreement – This is a fantastic option for a personal income tax debt that is less than $10,000. Don't hire a tax debt resolution professional to handle this type of agreement on your behalf... you are more than capable of addressing it on your own with some basic guidance. You typically only need to call the 800 number on the last notice received and ask for a "Guaranteed Installment Agreement." Remember that with this type of agreement, the total debt owed, plus estimated interest and penalties, must be paid within three years. Your payments shouldn't be more than about $350.00 per month.

- Streamlined Installment Agreement – This option is available to both individual income tax accounts and business tax debts if the business is no longer in operation. The threshold for this agreement is that the total assessed debt cannot be more than $50,000, and the debt must be paid in full within 72 months. This is the stage where I recommend you consider getting a tax debt resolution professional involved, especially if it's a business tax account debt or the total debt owed is closer to $50,000 than $20,000. There are too many places where this type of agreement could go sideways if you don't have the experience to watch out for pitfalls.

- In-Business Trust Fund Express – This agreement option is only available to existing business accounts with a balance of $25,000 or less, but carries a 24-month repayment term requirement. It's an excellent option for a simple "do it yourself" negotiation, but make sure the business is 100% compliant moving forward, or you could be opening Pandora's box.

- In-Business Installment Agreement – Only available to businesses and stipulates that the tax debt must be fully paid before the Collection Statute Expiration Date (CSED) lapses. Given the size of the debts owed for this type of agreement, you will run into personal assessment requirements for any portion of the tax debt that stems from past-due payroll taxes. For this reason, I would recommend you lean on an experienced tax debt resolution professional to handle it.

- Partial Payment Installment Agreement – This is one of the stickiest types of agreements to negotiate with the IRS and one I would suggest you not attempt on your own. Individuals and businesses can request this type of agreement, but to qualify, you have to prove to the IRS that you cannot be expected to pay the entire balance owed before the collection timeframe for the IRS expires. There will be a lot of scrutiny of any financial statement the IRS will require you to submit before this type of agreement can be finalized.

- Non-Streamlined Installment Agreement – This is the IRS's largest standardized option. This type of agreement is available for individuals with an assessed balance totaling less than $250,000, and the entire debt must be paid within the Collection Statute Expiration Date. With this type of agreement, your monthly payments will be somewhere in the neighborhood of $3,000-3,500 if you owe $249,999 and have ten years left on the collection statute, depending on the interest rates charged. If this is your tax account situation, hire a tax debt resolution professional to handle it for you. They may have better options and be more skilled with the negotiations required to ensure you get the best deal possible.

- Financial-based Installment Agreement – If your situation does not apply to any of those standardized options listed, this is a catch-all agreement established based on your current financial condition and the total debt owed. It has no specified timeframe that dictates the monthly payments or a debt limit attached.

State Options

As I have mentioned throughout this book, every single state handles its tax collection accounts differently. Some have strict Installment Agreement plans that only allow you to address a past-due tax debt over twelve months. Others allow you to pay over ten years if you can prove using a financial disclosure statement that you can't pay more than you are proposing. Do your research! And if it's something that you can't handle or simply don't want to, find an experienced tax debt resolution professional to handle it for you.

Key Points to Remember for All Installment Agreements

1. No matter if your Installment Agreement is set up for your personal or business tax account or if it is with the IRS or state, you MUST stay compliant with all tax obligations moving forward. Failure to remain compliant will cause the agreement

to default, and you will be back at square one.

2. If you are on an Installment Agreement and facing a problem where you will be late with a tax payment or filing obligation, call the tax agency *before* the deadline to let them know. You are typically granted one hiccup as long as you are communicating with the respected agency before the deadline. If you aren't proactive, you could be hit with a whammy and have to start the entire negotiation process from square one again.

3. If tax liens have not been filed against you yet, the terms of the agreement may require one to be filed. Ask questions when speaking with the tax agency or your tax debt resolution professional before any final terms are agreed upon. It is always best to prevent one from being filed if you are in the position to do so.

4. Financial disclosure statements are typically required for any Installment Agreement negotiation unless it is for a lower-balance tax debt and you are setting up the payments to be made over a short period of time. You will need to provide your financials for any extended agreement and, most certainly, for any agreement that would have you only paying a portion of the balance owed. Yes, they will scrutinize your bank accounts and how you spend your money. It can be uncomfortable! However, if the goal is to ask for their cooperation with not demanding full payment up front, sometimes you have to jump through some hoops.

5. In most cases, penalties will continue to be assessed until they reach the maximum threshold, and interest will continue to accrue until the tax debt reaches a zero balance. Keep this in mind when you call the tax agency and ask to pay your $30,000 debt with monthly payments of $100. It's like a high-interest credit card… if you only pay the minimum balance, you will be paying on the debt for years, and it won't go anywhere.

6. As long as you remain in contact with the tax agency and meet

all the deadlines they demand of you, all aggressive collection tactics will be placed on hold. No bank account levies, no wage garnishments, and no asset seizures.

7. Once you agree to an Installment Agreement, it is set in stone. Unless dire circumstances shift your financial condition for the worse, you will be required to meet the terms established without fail.

8. The IRS and most states charge a set-up fee for finalizing an Installment Agreement. If you ask, they should be able to take it out of your first payment.

Look Out For Your Own Best Interest If You Are Going to DIY Your Agreement

A potential client called me to inquire about my firm's services. Mary was in her early 70s, retired, and had a minor tax consequence because she worked full-time for a few years while collecting Social Security. The IRS was hounding her over a $12,000 balance she owed for tax years 2017, 2018, and 2019. She told me that when she called the IRS, they were demanding $620.00 per month payments, and she couldn't afford it with her limited income. She was near tears because she was so distraught! She wanted to hire me to negotiate with the IRS on her behalf.

The first thing I told her was, "Mary, you shouldn't hire me or anybody else to handle this for you." I walked Mary through the Streamlined Installment Agreement option. I walked her through the calculations required for the maximum repayment threshold of 72 months, which was almost one-third of what the agent on the phone was demanding she agree to. I also coached her on making sure they agreed not to file a tax lien because "Under the terms of the Streamlined Installment Agreement program, because my debt is below $25,000, you are not required to file one." By the time I got off the phone call with Mary, she was full of sass and confidence.

Mary called me the next day to thank me for helping her with the situation. She reported that she got on the phone with a "very helpful young man" at the IRS, and when she started walking him through her request for a Streamlined Installment Agreement, he didn't push back at all.

Summary

If you understand the tax law, the IRS and states will not be able to push you around. Get ahead of their collection process, and *you* will manage your cash flow instead of some voice on the other end of the phone deciding how much you will be allowed to get by on.

As you might imagine, figuring out how to save your assets and make the tax settlement as painless as possible requires strategic planning and an understanding of the collection process. Be realistic about whether your situation can be handled on your own with the help of this book and other resources, or if it would be wiser to lean on an experienced tax debt resolution professional to take over. There is *ALWAYS* a solution… make sure you hedge your bets to get the best one available to you!

Chapter 13:

Can You Pay Your Debt at 10 Cents on the Dollar?

My simple answer may frustrate some of you: "Sometimes."

The Offer in Compromise(OIC program, or Offer in Settlement program as some states refer to it, is where we make an offer to settle the total taxes owed based on your current financial condition.

Those Crazy Phone Salesmen

Over the last several decades, tax resolution mills have taken advantage of taxpayers, promising a resolution akin to the stars and the moon: the Offer in Compromise. Slick talkers will explain that the IRS and states will negotiate the total debt owed if only the taxpayer pays them $X,XXX to file their Power of Attorney and get the paperwork started.

If you receive this type of phone call, stop, take a deep breath, and think about it. An Offer in Compromise or Settlement proposal requires a full financial disclosure. Most often, these settlements are based on the equity you have accrued in your assets and your income versus what is deemed "allowable" expenses for your family size and geographic location. How in the world would a salesman know that you could qualify for an Offer in Compromise, and how did they know you have a tax debt???

The Coveted Tax Lien List

Once the IRS or state files a tax lien, the lien becomes a public record. There are thousands of "list" companies in the United States, and some of their top sellers are lists of taxpayers with tax liens filed against them. As soon as your name pops up, it becomes a valuable commodity; the list compiler will sell it to dozens of 800-number salesmen the same day the lien is recorded.

In turn, those salesmen start hammering the phone within minutes with scary predictions and high-pressure sales tactics. When they call you, they immediately start talking about the Offer in Compromise, hoping that the idea of an easy way out will be enough to get $5,000 or more out of you in the next few minutes.

While some of their pie-in-the-sky promises could come true, most often, they do not. We've had many clients contact us after paying retainers to these types of companies just to find out that one letter was sent to the IRS or state, and nothing else was done. Sometimes, an Offer in Compromise packet was sent to the clients, telling them to fill it out and providing instructions on where to mail it. Let me be very clear: that is NOT ethical or professional tax debt resolution.

The Offer in Compromise process is long, often taking up to a year to get an initial ruling; in many situations, those phone salesmen are long gone by then. One year later, you could find yourself in a bigger tax debt situation thanks to the ongoing accrual of penalties and interest and back at square one.

Ten cents on the dollar sounds great coming from a salesman pitching you on hiring his company, but as the age-old adage says, "If it sounds too good to be true, it usually is."

Is the Offer In Compromise Concept a Hoax?

I've had a lot of clients, and even other tax professionals, ask this same question of me. No, the Offer in Compromise programs are not a hoax. Using these programs, I have successfully negotiated settlements for hundreds of taxpayers over the years. They are definitely not easy to secure, but I am successful with them because I know when it is appropriate to use this resolution option for a client and, more importantly, when not to.

The Offer in Compromise (hereafter referred to simply as "OIC") is the most common request I get from those who owe the IRS or state, so I'll give you a lot of insight into how it all works.

Here are the OIC program's good, bad, and ugly. Then, we'll go into the details of how to get one approved:

The Good:

- An OIC can provide a fresh start from your IRS or state tax debts. It's especially effective if you owe more than $50,000.

- The OIC will allow you to realize significant savings when paying the tax debt because, in most cases, the debt is settled for a mere fraction of the total balance owed. This is where the "pennies on the dollar" notion came from.

- An OIC can be submitted to address any tax owed to the IRS: income, payroll, unemployment, etc.

- If you disagree with the results of the first-tier review and negotiations, you typically have the right to appeal the decision and take the proposal to a secondary reviewer.

- There will be no more worrying about the IRS or state seizing your wages or bank accounts while the OIC is considered and once finalized, as long as you remain compliant with the terms negotiated.

- Improved credit score - Following the payment of an accepted OIC, the IRS and/or state will release the tax liens that had previously been filed, and your credit report will state that the debts have been satisfied.

- While the compromise is under consideration, IRS and state collections are halted. After approval, you will be free of IRS and state collection notices, Revenue Officer visits, and wondering what's next.

- Once the OIC has been approved, it is a "final negotiation" that cannot be changed unless you do something to default its terms. You can even win the lottery the month after the official acceptance, and it won't change your settlement.

- You've put the past due tax debt and all collection worries behind you. Finally, you can sleep at night without worrying about what they might do to you next. It's over.

The Bad:

- You will still have to pay something towards the past-due taxes, but the amount is based on your assets and net income after allowable expenses are considered.

- The IRS or state will push for the highest settlement amount possible. Often, their initial calculations are absurdly different than what you propose. This is intentional!

- Under penalty of perjury, you must provide full financial disclosure to the tax agencies. This includes telling them where you work, where you bank, and what assets you have.

- They are going to go over your financials with a fine-tooth comb. Remember, they already know 95% of what is happening in America (and most times offshore), so it is best practice to plan for a full and open financial disclosure.

- The IRS ten-year clock to collect on each tax period is paused. The pause goes into effect the day the IRS receives the OIC and doesn't end until a final acceptance or rejection is determined. Most states follow similar practices.

- If the IRS or state accepts your OIC, it comes with strings attached. With the IRS, you commit to remaining in full tax obligation compliance for at least five years; the states with OIC programs typically follow similar rules.

- Not all 50 states utilize an OIC/Offer in Settlement program; if offered, not all types of taxes can be compromised.

The Ugly:

- An OIC is not a quick cure; it can take the IRS 6-9 months to respond with an initial assessment of the proposal, then another 3-9 months to finalize depending on the additional financial information requested and negotiations required. With most state programs, it moves a bit faster, with an estimated initial response of 60-90 days and another 3-9 months to finalize.

- Unless you have decided to retain an experienced tax debt resolution professional to handle this, you can easily get beaten up by the IRS or state during the negotiation part of an OIC. This is simply because the rules of the "game" are vast and convoluted.

- You must be in full tax compliance to submit an OIC. All tax returns must be on record (even if it is an SFR compiled by the IRS or state), and you must be tending to all ongoing tax obligations without fail. One slip-up will cause the OIC to be returned without consideration.

- If you are untruthful about your income or assets during the application process, you commit a felony due to the "penalty of perjury" clause outlined in the program documentation.

- The IRS and states are incredibly cheap regarding the expenses allowed taxpayers to tend to their health and welfare. While there may be a bit of wiggle room, their expectations align with the latest findings of the US Census Bureau, the American Community Survey, and Bureau of Labor Statistics Data reports. For example, at the time of writing this book, the "allowed" Housing and Utilities expense for a family of three in Los Angeles County was $3,486; in reality, that amount *may* cover the rent of a two-bedroom apartment. This is when it pays to have an experienced tax debt resolution professional involved because the OIC program allows for negotiation… within reason, of course.

- If the IRS or state determines you have assets that could clear the debt, even though it may be the equity in your residence, they will reject the offer proposed.

- The IRS and states do not care about fairness; their job is to collect as much money as possible from you. The OIC will be rejected if they believe other collection processes will net them more cash.

- Approximately 80% of all OICs proposed are rejected. While there are various reasons for the rejections, the predominant cause is that the taxpayer simply did not qualify to settle the debt. This is, again, why you should engage an experienced tax debt resolution professional who has been through the OIC process more than just a handful of times.

- One missed tax payment or unfiled return could cause the OIC to officially default. When this happens, the entire debt, minus the payments made under the OIC terms, is recorded back on your tax account with an addition: all the penalties and interest that should have been charged while the OIC was in place.

- Though the state programs may dictate other terms, with the IRS, if you are granted an OIC, you must remain in full tax compliance for at least five years after the OIC is finalized. Failure to do so will cause the entire debt, minus the payments made towards the settlement figure, plus all penalties and interest that should have been charged. There are LONG-term requirements for these types of settlements!

Most taxpayers don't expect to get off scot-free; they want to catch up on the taxes, but the tax bill is so big that it has become impossible to get in front of. With the added penalties and interest, it's a snowball that gets bigger and bigger as it rolls down a huge hill. This is why the OIC programs were developed: they provide a legal avenue to settle the debt when there is no other way the taxpayer can address it. The IRS and most states know it is better to cut their losses and get what they can instead of wasting resources on unproductive collection attempts.

An Example of How the OIC Worked for One Client

I had a client in California, Georgina, who was self-employed as a real estate agent. She contacted me about a tax debt issue with the IRS that needed to be addressed: taxes owed for 2011, 2012, 2013, 2014, 2015, 2016, 2017, and 2018, with missing returns for 2019 and 2020. The IRS was threatening to levy her bank accounts and file substitute tax returns for the missing years, so she knew she needed help.

I immediately contacted the IRS and negotiated a stay of any enforced collection actions to give us breathing room to pull together the missing returns. Once those were filed, Georgina's tax debt totaled over $220,000.

After doing a complete financial analysis of her assets and how the IRS would consider her income versus expenses, I found that the Offer in Compromise program would be ideal to bring a final resolution to the tax account. We proposed an initial settlement amount of $7,323.34.

An Offer Examiner was assigned, and after sending updated documentation showing Georgina's financial activities between the time the OIC was submitted and the review date, the Offer Examiner responded with a determination that the settlement amount should be increased to $47,490.60. Remember, it is their job to push back on any proposed settlement… they want to collect every possible dollar they can to be applied to the debt.

Upon reviewing the Offer Examiner's calculations supporting the $47,490.60 figure, I called Georgina and filled her in. It was still a great reduction in the debt, which was then sitting at $231,039.26, but Georgina was still devastated. There was no way she could ever afford to pay over $47,000 back within the 24 months the program allowed, which I knew and had a plan to address. "Sit tight… I have more negotiating to do. I just wanted you to know that we are making progress!" I told her.

I went back to the proverbial drawing board and began picking apart the Offer Examiner's calculations. I found that she had included in her calculations assets that belonged to Georgina's boyfriend, she did not include costs allowable for the addition of the daughter Georgina had while the Offer in Compromise was waiting to be reviewed, and the Examiner had reduced Georgina's housing and utility expenses to 50% of what she actually paid. As a result of these findings and my subsequent negotiations with the Offer Examiner, we settled the OIC at a final figure of $9,973.00. It took some muscle, but we got it done!

Georgina is a prime example of when the OIC program is a great solution. She worked hard to pay the OIC settlement within five months of its approval, has remained fully compliant with her ongoing tax filing and payment obligations, and has been saving up to purchase her first home.

Having a tax debt puts some people on a lifelong downward spiral. Georgina took it as an opportunity to learn how to tend to her tax obligations, and as soon as she got the OIC addressed, she started working toward building a solid and financially stable home for her and her daughter.

Some may argue with me when I say this, but I have witnessed it play out thousands of times with my client's cases: though the IRS and states want to collect as much money as possible towards a tax debt, they don't want to destroy you. They want you to learn their version of the golden rule: always tend to your tax obligations and address a debt if one is on the books. Once that is achieved, they want you to go on living a productive and stable life. Georgina will be a model citizen moving forward because the OIC program let her settle her debt and move on.

And take heed: if you successfully address your tax debt through a settlement program with the IRS or state, do everything within your capabilities to uphold the terms. The OIC is seen as a second chance… the tax agencies aren't interested in giving you a third.

The Three Types of OIC Options With the IRS

The IRS' OIC program has three different reasons for a settlement to be considered:

- Doubt as to Collectibility
- Doubt as to Liability
- Effective Tax Administration

Though almost all of the OIC petitions I have submitted to the IRS for my clients have been based on Doubt as to Collectibility (the taxpayer doesn't have the financial capabilities to address the debt), it's important to understand the basis for the other two options.

Doubt as to Liability allows the taxpayer to say to the IRS, "You have determined that I owe taxes, but I truly don't, and here's why…" Remember that the burden of proof to support this challenge rests firmly on the shoulders of the taxpayer. The IRS will want proof (or disproof) of income and/or proof that any disallowed deduction, expense claimed, or credits taken were legitimate.

The Effective Tax Administration OIC program can be summarized with the following statement: "I owe the tax, and I have the means to

101

pay it, but it would be unfair for the IRS to demand me to do so." This is the most challenging type of OIC to get approved by the IRS because it is all up to the interpretation of the agents who are unlucky enough to be assigned. Per the Internal Revenue Manual, there must be exceptional circumstances or "compelling" public policy or equity consideration that provide a sufficient basis for this type of compromise to be made.

If I did a deep dive into the OIC program options for you, I could fill a 300-page book. Because I am simply providing an overview of resolution options that help you understand that there is *ALWAYS* a solution, I will stick to an overarching, 20,000-foot view. Therefore, we will focus solely on the basics of the most common type: the IRS Doubt as to Collectibility OIC.

How to Qualify for a Doubt as to Collectibility IRS OIC

You will not qualify for the OIC program if you have other means of paying your taxes or can address the taxes owed through an Installment Agreement. However, it may be a viable option if you don't have the assets to pay the bill or if it would create severe financial hardship for your family. The IRS Offer Specialist will negotiate with you or your tax debt resolution professional what severe hardship means.

Your goal is to try to get your settlement as low as possible, but know the tax agencies have little tolerance for renting a cabin on the lake over the summer or a new Range Rover. So, if you think an OIC is an ideal solution to your tax problem, start making strategic financial decisions now. You may need to dial back your lifestyle for the next few years, but saving 60-90% on your tax bill will be worth it.

Just because you petition the IRS with an OIC proposal does not mean you'll get approved. Only 20% of the offers submitted are accepted, but there is a valid reason for this low figure... more on that later in this chapter. Proposing an offer starts the IRS on a process of verification and examination to fully understand the taxpayer's financial limitations and any specific circumstances that may further affect payment.

When an OIC proposal is appropriate, it provides a solution to not only the taxpayer but to the tax agency as well. If the taxpayer has no means to address the total tax bill owed, there is no sense in the government applying more resources to fruitless efforts. It's better to get something applied to the debt with a promise from the taxpayer that he/she will remain in full tax compliance moving forward.

The eligibility requirements

For a Doubt as to Collectibility OIC, the requirements are pretty basic:

- You must have a filing on record for every tax year (yes, even a substitute filing compiled by the IRS counts).

- You must be compliant with any current tax payment obligations.

- You must provide a complete financial disclosure statement (Form 433-A OIC at the time of this writing) and sign it under penalty of perjury.

- You must submit months of supporting documentation proving the information provided on the financial disclosure statement (copies of bank account statements, household bills, etc.).

- Unless you qualify for the low-income certification threshold stipulated on the OIC form, you must submit a processing fee and a first payment towards the proposed settlement amount.

- You cannot be actively pursuing bankruptcy protection.

Before proposing an OIC to address your tax debt, you should also ensure that any lingering innocent spouse claims, or open tax audits are cleared.

Please note that if your OIC is denied or withdrawn, the funds submitted to the IRS in compliance with the proposal will be applied to the past-due taxes owed, not returned to you.

Financial evaluation of an OIC proposal

Offers are approved based on an examination of the applicant's particular set of facts and circumstances, which include:

- Amount of the taxpayer's average monthly income,
- The total monthly allowable expenses, and
- The taxpayer's equity in assets.

These numbers determine how much equity you amassed in assets while the tax debt was accruing and how much disposable income you have on a monthly basis for application to the tax debt.

The RCP or Reasonable Collection Potential

When you submit an OIC to the IRS, they expect you to submit a reasonable offer based on your current financial condition and limited ability to pay toward the past-due tax debt. When they receive an offer proposal, they will run their own numbers, and if your offer is lower than they determine you could pay, they will provide their calculations as a challenge to the initial proposal. If the taxpayer does not respond and open the negotiation phase of the OIC's consideration, the Offer Examiner will reject the proposal.

> **NOTE**: The first financial evaluation provided in response to your OIC request will almost always show that you can somehow, miraculously, fully pay the debt. They do this on purpose... do not get discouraged!

The negotiation phase of an OIC proposal can be viewed in three ways: a healthy negotiation where you dissect the calculations made by the Offer Examiner and challenge their findings with documented proof that they are incorrect, agree to some of their calculations and challenge others, or agree to their findings and agree to the new offer figure (which 99% of the time is significantly higher than your initial proposal). Because most people who submit OIC proposals to the IRS do not understand this, they take that first challenge as the final word and don't think there are any other options; this is why only 20% of OIC petitions are accepted.

How Do They Come Up with a Dollar Figure?

The IRS determines the legitimacy of your offer based solely on your financial condition. They start with your business and personal balance sheet and add up your equity in bank accounts, life insurance, real estate, automobiles, business equipment, jewelry, art, and everything else that might be sold.

> **Just a hint:** double-check your insurance policies for any "extras" you have coverage for. I once had a client hit with an increase in asset value during the OIC negotiations because she had a piece of art insured for $25,000 that she didn't disclose to me!

Then, they consider your income. If you're making $200,000 a year, they will not consider an offer of $500 a month. Though the Offer Examiners know they can't get blood from a turnip, they will figure out how to whittle your finances down to include every single penny possible in the settlement figure. This is where your decision to retain an experienced tax debt resolution professional could make or break you; he/she will ingest the first response from the IRS, gather updated records from you, and then start picking apart their calculations line by line.

The Simple Equations the IRS Uses for an OIC

QSV = Quick Sell Value is 80% of the asset's fair market value minus consideration for any loan balance outstanding. Since the current market value of everything these days is so volatile, there may be some extra wiggle room that can be negotiated.

NDI = Net Disposable Income is the money left over after paying for your necessary health and welfare expenses each month. Remember that what they view as "necessary" expenses for you doesn't always align with what you think should be recognized as necessary.

An experienced tax debt resolution professional with hundreds of hours of experience debating income, expenses, and equity in assets with Offer Examiners should be well-versed in preparing for entering this negotiation phase and successfully maneuvering through it.

Lump-Sum Cash Offer: The simple formula for a lump-sum offer, which means the settlement amount is paid in five months or less after official acceptance, is:

$$QSV + NDI \text{ multiplied by } 12$$

This means that the total they will accept is the quick sale value of your assets plus your leftover income for the next year. Now, I'm sure you see the potential for failure here. They want you to pay your monthly installment based on 12 months of income, but you must pay the balance of the accepted settlement within five months of getting your acceptance letter. Keep that in mind while negotiating your OIC.

Also, remember that in the lump sum cash offer, you must include a check for 20% of your offer as the first payment; if the OIC is rejected, they will keep your 20% and apply it to your tax debt.

Periodic Payment Offer: The formula used to calculate what would be acceptable under this type of OIC proposal is:

QSV + NDI multiplied by 24

This method necessitates adding the quick sale value of your assets to your leftover monthly income multiplied by 24. If you go with this type of offer, unless you qualify for the Low-Income Certification, you must immediately start making the monthly payments (no 20% down), even though they have not approved your request. If your offer is rejected, they keep your payments, of course.

I always analyze both options before making an offer so my clients can evaluate the benefits and risks of each, as should any other experienced tax debt resolution professional you may retain.

My Success Rate with the OIC Program

I have been successful with OIC petitions for my clients because I know how the IRS will interpret a financial statement that serves as the backbone of an OIC.

When I review my client's financial statements, I look at them with the same type of scrutiny the IRS will, and use it to prequalify my client for the best resolution option possible. If it's the OIC, when I submit the packet to the IRS, I anticipate aggressive negotiations will be necessary because it's standard procedure. However, we usually settle close to the offer amount I initially calculated and proposed. I say this with a HUGE asterisk attached… let me explain:

A client came to me with very clean records that supported him being a perfect OIC candidate. He had minimal equity in assets that would be considered appropriate for his income level. When I looked over his bank statements, no unreasonable expenses were showing up. He had minimal credit cards with low revolving balances, his monthly income was near his monthly allowable expenses, and he had a reasonable vehicle with minimal equity. He had a small investment account with a low balance and wasn't contributing much to it monthly. Everything looked great! We submitted an OIC for around $5,000 to settle a past-due IRS tax balance of over $75,000 from his younger, wilder, and more irresponsible years.

The first response we received from the Offer Examiner pushed back a bit on us with a counteroffer of around $9,500. While we were gathering our records to respond, I got a call from the Offer Examiner saying, "We've got a problem."

It turns out that the taxpayer failed to disclose to me and on the financial statement he signed under penalty of perjury that he was the beneficiary of a trust and his rights to the funds were going to be disbursed to him at age 30. He was 28 when we began the OIC process, meaning he would have access to the money soon. The Offer Examiner found out through a loan application the taxpayer had previously submitted to his bank but failed to disclose to me.

The lesson from this story is two-fold:

- One: if you work with a tax debt resolution professional to handle your past-due tax debt, think of that person as a priest/ probation officer/parent... confess every detail, no matter how embarrassing or insignificant you may think it is. Without disclosing everything that could have an impact, he or she will be unable to be 100% effective in pursuing a resolution for you.

- Two: the IRS (and states) can sniff out more than you think. It is always best to be honest, open, and upfront about everything as you seek a resolution to a past-due tax debt. It prevents everyone from wasting time and prevents you from spending money on a resolution that may not come about due to a technicality.

Either way, if I pre-qualify you as a candidate for the program, we will ask the IRS to take a big haircut with the Offer in Compromise. If we play it right and are honest with your ability to pay, you have an excellent chance for approval.

What If They Reject My Offer?

If the IRS rejects the initial offer proposal, that's not the final answer! As mentioned previously, this is a negotiation, and we have appeal rights. Depending on why the Offer Examiner decided to reject the OIC, we may exercise those rights and ask for the OIC to be submitted to a different division, the Appeals Unit, for further consideration.

If the Offer Examiner's reason for rejecting the OIC is sound and it's found that appealing the decision won't get us anywhere, we'll turn to other alternatives to address the debt.

What Are the Long-Term Consequences?

This question generally concerns getting back to your quest for building financial security. With an accepted OIC, as long as you make your agreed-upon payments and tend to your tax obligations without fail moving forward, you have no further worries where the IRS (or state) is concerned.

My experience has been that once the tax debt is off the table, you'll become a better money manager. Most of my clients recover in a few years and are back on track, but they are on solid ground this time.

The second question is, "What about my credit report?" Because tax liens are no longer considered a part of your consumer credit score and report, there should be no impact on your ability to secure a credit card or vehicle loan. With respect to a mortgage or high-dollar loan application, the tax debt will be reflected as "satisfied."

Summary of the OIC Program

The OIC program is a great way to settle your past-due tax debts if you qualify for it. As with all things having to do with taxes, there are a lot of rules that surround it. However, it could be worth your while:

Advantages

- You end up paying back only a portion of the total tax debt owed.

- An OIC allows any tax liens filed against the taxpayer to be removed faster than other resolution options.

- Savings are realized with a final amount to pay that will not accrue penalties or interest.

Disadvantages

- Unless you qualify for the Low-Income Certification, you must pay a filing fee to process the request. It's a relatively minor amount, but it needs to be paid.

- You have to make payments towards the debt, with the final terms being unknown until the negotiations are concluded and a settlement number is determined.

- You have to disclose all aspects of your finances.

- In most cases, the time clock that keeps track of how long the IRS has to collect on the debt gets paused.

- There is a possibility of the IRS rejecting the request.

- You must be perfectly tax-compliant for five years following the OIC's acceptance.

If you want to learn more about the IRS' directives about how they evaluate an Offer in Compromise proposal, go to your internet search engine and type in the following:

IRS Internal Revenue Manual Part 5.8

This section within the IRS' ruling guidebook outlines exactly how Offer Examiners are instructed to evaluate an OIC for acceptance. It's dry... I'll warn you of that now! But, if you want to get a peek behind the curtain at the IRS, this is a great place to start.

Chapter 14:

Is Getting the IRS or State to Forgive Penalties Possible?

One of the easier ways to reduce the total debt you need to pay back to the IRS or state is to request that the penalties assessed be forgiven, or "abated," as the process is referred to in the tax world. And yes, if your situation warrants it, the IRS or state *will* grant this type of reduction on your account through the Penalty Abatement or Tax Penalty Waiver programs. To get the best results with this type of request, you must first understand why the tax agencies charge penalties.

The Reason the IRS and States Assess Penalties

The tax agencies charge penalties to discourage taxpayers from failing to meet their ongoing tax obligations. With the knowledge that every time a return is filed late or a tax deposit is paid late, extra money will be added to the bill, most taxpayers will do everything they possibly can to prevent those charges from being added. It's a proverbial rap with a ruler on the back of your knuckles.

And, as a byproduct of charging these penalties, the tax agencies make more money. For tax filing season 2022, the IRS processed over 164,000,000 returns. If every single one of them were charged just an extra $100 in penalties by the IRS and the taxpayers paid it, the IRS would generate over $16,400,000,000 in excess revenues. That's a whole lot of zeroes!

> **Note:** To prevent excessive penalties from being charged, *always* file your tax returns on time, even if you can't afford to pay the taxes owed on them. Late filing penalties can be assessed for up to 25% of any unpaid tax owed!

Before we get into the process of submitting the request, it's best to review how to qualify for a penalty abatement. You have to start by disclosing to the IRS and state why you couldn't meet your tax obligations: "I couldn't file and pay my taxes on time because…" The barometer usually used is referred to as "reasonable cause."

What is "Reasonable Cause?"

Reasonable cause is anything outside your control that caused you to be unable to file your tax return or pay on time. Keep in mind that the reason behind the tax issues has to be something significant. Tales such as "I had to pay my kid's college tuition" or "Our dog ate our tax return paperwork" aren't likely to get a positive result.

While the specifics of what is classified as "reasonable cause" are considered on a case-by-case basis, the IRS and states have some general guidelines of what falls into this category:

- Death or serious illness,
- Unavoidable absence of the taxpayer,
- Destruction of records due to fire, natural cause, or other qualifying casualties,
- Erroneous error or advice by a CPA, Bookkeeper, or Tax Return Preparer,
- There are errors on the IRS or State's part, and more.

Though these are the primary and most common reasons the IRS or state will consider a Penalty Abatement or Waiver, other explanations and circumstances can be considered.

A client came to me with a pretty sad situation that immediately made me think, "They deserve a Penalty Abatement." Karen's dad had dementia for the last few years of his life, and upon his death, she and her brothers found that his tax returns for 2016, 2017, 2018, and 2019 hadn't been filed or paid. He had been pretty wealthy, always having paid quarterly estimated tax payments for the income he was receiving from significant investments and retirement vehicles that paid for his living expenses, so she knew there would be some consequences.

After working with a CPA to get the missing returns compiled, Karen and her brothers oversaw their dad's estate, pay the principal taxes owed to the tune of over $85,000 to the IRS and $34,000 to the state. Once the returns were filed and paid, notices started flying from the IRS and state about the penalties and interest owed, amounting to over $49,000 in extra charges that needed to be addressed.

I outlined in a lengthy dissertation the truth about their dad's situation: he had been diagnosed with the onset of dementia in 2014, and it slowly progressed over the years. In March of 2017, he became disoriented and fell down a flight of stairs, ending up in the hospital for several weeks, which was the start of a rapid decline. Due to that fall, he didn't file his 2016 return, and his quarterly estimated tax payments stopped being paid.

Following his release from the hospital, the symptoms caused by his dementia became much worse, and he declined to the point where he couldn't form coherent sentences. Though his mind was slowly going, his body was in peak physical condition, which is how he lived as long as he did under the constant care of nurses and caretakers. Though Karen and her brothers would take turns coming to stay with their dad, they all had families and lived out of town, so it was a constant juggle. Their dad's banker and financial advisor oversaw all the monthly finances for their dad and his recurring, auto-drafted bills, so the last thing on any of their minds were the finances or tax obligations.

Once we explained this situation to the IRS and the state, we were asked to justify her Dad's medical condition during the years in question with records from the doctors and caretakers. It didn't take long after submitting those records for us to receive full abatement of the penalties charged, along with the interest that had been charged related to the penalty balances. It was the right thing for the tax agencies to do! There had been no ill intent by anyone or any perceived tax evasion to be found... Karen's dad just didn't have the mental capacity because of the disease to tend to his tax obligations.

How Do I Apply for a Penalty Abatement/Waiver?

The strongest penalty abatement requests will always tie the tax debt accrued directly to the events that caused it. If the penalty abatement is for your personal tax account, it's a straightforward request. You simply outline what happened and how it impacted your tax responsibilities.

For example, let's say your home office is in your basement, and your sewer line backed up, destroying all your financial records in April of 2022. This event could have impacted your 2021 tax return filing, your records kept for the first few months of 2022, and payment of any self-employment tax payments due in April for the 2022 tax year. It may even bleed into covering any tax payments not made for the following few months as you pay for the necessary repairs to your home. What you couldn't claim was included in this event is if you failed to pay your taxes throughout the 2021 tax year because they were due before the flooding happened. It's pretty easy to follow if you think about it.

You'll be held to a higher standard if you want to submit a penalty abatement for a business tax account. Extra consideration of whether you employed "ordinary business care and prudence" will come into play. As a business owner, you can't say, "Well, I thought my secretary was paying the payroll taxes as I told her she needed to." That just won't fly as a plausible excuse in the eyes of the IRS or state because there didn't appear to be any checks or balances as expected if you were responsibly running your business.

Don't expect a swift response when you submit a penalty abatement request. These are often the most dreaded type of request for someone at the IRS or state to get saddled with because it is so subjective. Every time an abatement is granted, it sets a precedent for consideration of other similar types of requests in the future. It's a slippery slope, and the tax agencies know it.

The IRS and state will review the request to issue a first-level determination of approval, partial approval, or denial. Most of the time, it's a flat-out "no." But don't fret; it's their job to try to reject your request! It wasn't your only shot at getting this type of reduction…

What Happens If the IRS or State Denies a Request for Penalty Abatement or Waiver of Penalties?

The IRS and most States allow an appeal of the denial of an abatement or waiver request.

In all my years of dealing with Penalty Abatement requests for my clients, 95% of them have been won at the appeals level, not during the first round of review. Why is this? Because they assume if you receive a "no" determination, you won't fight it. If you have a sound basis for pointing the finger at an event or situation that rationally caused the tax problems, *do not take the first "no" as the absolute and final answer!*

When you push back on the IRS or state with an appeal of their first review and rejection of your request for penalty relief, it goes to a different group of reviewers. Usually, these individuals have more tenure with the tax agencies and more latitude with what they can consider. These are the people you can actually reason with!

If the IRS or State approves or partially approves the request, a notice will be issued, and the account will be adjusted accordingly. In addition to penalties being reduced or removed after approval or partial approval, any interest associated with the penalty amount assessed will also be reduced.

Summary

Penalty Abatements and Waivers are not handed out like candy by the IRS and states, but can be granted. If you have a situation you believe warrants the penalties being abated, and it's less than a few thousand dollars, give it a go. If the penalties have really added up and the reason you accrued the debt is sticky, get an experienced tax debt resolution professional involved. We know the best angles to use when approaching these types of requests. It's not a science-backed process, so know that it's a bit of a gamble. But I'd rather roll the dice and spend a few thousand chasing the relief of $40,000, wouldn't you?

Chapter 15:

What About Filing for Bankruptcy?

Should you file for bankruptcy and let it all work out in the courts?

First of all, I want you to know that bankruptcy is complicated, and you will not be able to make a decision based only on the information in this chapter. There are literally volumes of law books that dictate how bankruptcies are to be handled, with each state having its subtle nuances. This is no DIY escape plan; it will be drawn out and expensive.

However, it is tempting because we have all heard of someone who filed for bankruptcy, got to keep their house and means of making a living, settled their debts for five or ten cents on the dollar paid over several years, and pretty soon everything seems to return to normal.

I will caution you to only resort to bankruptcy if it is the ONLY option available to you based on the total debts you have. If your only debt aside from a few small balance credit cards is your tax bill, there will always be a better option than bankruptcy. Remember, there is *ALWAYS* a solution. Don't panic. Make thoughtful decisions going forward, and you'll be back on top in a few years.

The moment you file bankruptcy, your credit score will drop by at least 200 points. The bankruptcy will stay on your public record for 7 to 10 years, affecting your future ability to get a mortgage or buy a car at a decent credit rating. Remember how I told you tax liens don't affect your consumer credit score? Bankruptcies do!

That doesn't necessarily mean you are dead in the water as you try to rebuild your financial fortress following bankruptcy. Many famous people have filed for bankruptcy and went on to recover: Walt Disney,

Milton Hershey, Burt Reynolds, 50 Cent, Kim Basinger, Mike Tyson, Meat Loaf, Wayne Newton, Abraham Lincoln, Mark Twain, Francis Ford Coppola, and others. Henry Ford even filed for bankruptcy *twice* before finally figuring out how to make cars at a profit.

I had a client come to me wanting a better resolution to an IRS tax debt than she currently had. Tish's debt to the IRS was only $37,000 for tax years 2015, 2016, 2017, 2018, and 2019, and she was making $400 per month payments towards it. I immediately began to think about evaluating the monthly payment amount and options like a Currently Not-Collectible status or OIC; however, my thought process changed the more she explained.

After further talking to Tish about her financial condition, I learned she had fallen into the trap of high-interest revolving payday loans and credit cards. All said, she had six payday loans with a total balance of $19,000 owed between them and over $16,000 in credit card debt. With a gross income each year of $52,000, she couldn't leverage any of her payments enough to get out from under this nasty debt cloud, and the interest was burying her. I suggested Tish meet with a bankruptcy attorney.

The first words out of her mouth were, "But you can't address income taxes through bankruptcy!"

There are a LOT of misconceptions about bankruptcy out there, this being one of them: you *can* address income taxes in bankruptcy as long as they are more than three years old. Whether they are discharged or payments are set up depends on the type of bankruptcy you file.

I referred Tish to a credible bankruptcy attorney, and after meeting with him, she found that my advisement had been correct. She filed for Chapter 7 bankruptcy and was able to move on from her debt headaches.

When should you use bankruptcy as a tax resolution strategy?

Generally, when you have a lot of debt sources, not just taxes alone, or if your tax debts are at least three years old. If your corporation has $75,000 in past-due income taxes and you're behind another $150,000 in debt to your vendors without the cash flow to carry that type of debt on your balance sheet, you may want to consider the bankruptcy route. If you are an individual with a lot of credit card debt, income tax debts owed to the IRS and state, you have little-to-no assets, and your income level barely keeps your head above water, it's a route that may be best for the reset you desire.

But, you should NEVER make this decision on your own. It is best to meet with a reputable bankruptcy attorney with a copy of all your outstanding bills, your last one or two years' tax returns, and recent income and expense records. Any bankruptcy attorney worth their salt will meet with you to assess the situation without any fee being required.

What Are the Most Common Types of Bankruptcies?

Chapter 7: This is the complete liquidation of all your assets. It's available for individuals as well as businesses. A court-appointed trustee will let you get out with your personal effects and reasonable assets needed for your health and welfare. Everything else goes to a bankruptcy trustee to sell at auction or to a liquidator. The cash raised is divided between all your creditors, including the IRS or state.

As an individual, you may be able to file bankruptcy for $5,000 to $10,000. Don't fall for the "we'll file your bankruptcy for $750!" ads… that is just the cost to file the paperwork, not for representing you through the process. If you're filing as a business, expect a significant cost. I've heard of more prominent corporate bankruptcies that have cost over a quarter-million. Those are the big corporations, so expect your business' costs to be somewhere in the $25,000 to $50,000 range. However, Chapter 7 bankruptcy is cheaper than a long drawn-out Chapter 11, where you try to save your business.

Chapter 11: This is for a business that wants to negotiate payments to creditors, predators, and tax collectors, also known as "reorganizing." Individuals with secured and unsecured debts totaling more than $2.75 million can also use this reorganizing plan.

The overarching idea for this type of bankruptcy is that the business continues operating and retains most of its assets while the debts are restructured into an affordable payment plan.

If you enter an Installment Agreement or Offer in Compromise resolution plan and then file bankruptcy, the negotiated settlements with the IRS will be null and void. So don't negotiate a lower tax bill, then file bankruptcy; it won't provide any benefit.

Chapter 13: It is the same as 11 but is only for individuals and sole proprietors with secured and unsecured debts below $2.75 million; all other business entity types must use Chapter 11. Sole proprietors can use Chapter 13 to bundle the business and personal debt into one all-encompassing bundle and work on reducing the entire thing.

> **Note:** Remember, payroll and sales tax debts cannot be discharged through bankruptcy, no matter if you are filing in the business' name or personally, to address the personal responsibility assessments. It just won't happen.

There are two times when you might choose to go bankrupt:

A. You have no hope of salvaging anything from your finances and need a clean slate to start over.

B. The creditors, predators, and tax collectors are closing in on all sides, and you need a little more time and some protection to sort it all out.

Who Should Do the Work for You?

If you are under attack (lawsuits, liens, levies, and garnishments), you may need to file a bankruptcy petition immediately to slow down the process. I know you've seen those ads on bus stop benches featuring an oversized head of some woman in a suit offering a "deal" for affordable bankruptcy filings. That level of representation is for those who defaulted on the loan for their TV and owed the cell phone carrier a few hundred dollars. If taxes are in the mix, do not turn to a TV or bus stop "preacher" in your hour of need. Do your homework and find someone reputable in the area. (If you need a referral, please get in touch with my office and we can help.)

Summary

Is bankruptcy right for you? I'm hoping the answer is no. It's expensive, can drag on for a long time, and the outcome is unpredictable because the judge will make the final decisions. Once they make a ruling, it requires an appeal to change their mind, which keeps the costs and emotional drains flowing.

You want to put all this behind you with as little damage as possible, but mostly, you want to get it done quickly. If you analyze your debt and financial situation and find that filing a bankruptcy petition is in your best interest, immediately meet with a reputable bankruptcy attorney. The longer you wait, the more risk you will put yourself or your company in for the situation to get worse.

Chapter 16:

The "I's" of Joint Tax Returns: Innocent Spouse vs. Injured Spouse

If you file a joint income tax return with someone, both parties are typically responsible for any taxes owed. However, as with most things with the IRS and state tax agencies, asterisks come into play: *if both parties are fully aware of all financial activities reported and if neither has a tax debt lingering from before the marriage.

Full disclosure here… in my practice, I typically only come across Innocent Spouse situations. This is because I represent clients with broader-scope tax account issues. Injured Spouse petitions are usually a one-time tax account issue that your local accountant or CPA can address with a petition submitted when filing a joint tax return in a proactive move to protect the innocent spouse.

Let's first look at the "if both parties are *not* fully aware of all financial activities reported" portion, also known as "Innocent Spouse Relief."

Timothy and Rebecca had been married for over fifteen years, living a quiet suburban life in Ohio. Timothy was a painter with a single-member LLC business, handling a lot of big jobs for professional athletes, the local university, and many of the larger businesses in the area. Becky worked as an IT specialist for a big company in the area and had a comfortable W-2 salary. The financial activities for Tim's painting business had always been reported on a Schedule C on their joint income tax return. While Becky had always been a bit irritated with Timothy's slack handling of his business' financial records, it had never caused a big problem. They always filed their tax returns jointly and never had a tax consequence… until now.

While matching 1099s reported by third parties, the IRS found an anomaly on Timothy and Rebecca's 2019 income tax return: the gross payments for 1099s reported as paid to Timothy's business totaled $670,000, but his tax return reported only $590,000. As such, a tax consequence for the underreporting of income was recorded.

Now, the timing of this event just so happened to occur in July of 2023, and Timothy and Rebecca's income tax return for 2022 had been under an extension but had been sent in at the end of June, with an expected refund owed of $7,200.00 thanks to Rebecca's steady withholding. You can probably read the tea leaves to determine what happened. Yes, the IRS confiscated the entire tax refund and applied it to the past-due taxes owed caused by Timothy's "loose" accounting. To say that Rebecca was fuming was an understatement!

Timothy reached out to me with his hat in hand, asking if anything could be done. He felt awful that the refund, which Rebecca had intended to use as a downpayment on a new car, was taken.

After calming Rebecca down and looking at her paystubs and the estimated tax payments Timothy had made throughout the year, it was clear to see that Rebecca's portion of income tax requirements was sufficiently addressed (and then some) by her income tax withheld. The whole issue surrounded Timothy's additional tax assessment for a forgotten 1099 received from a local restaurant chain for which his business had done some work.

We filed an Innocent Spouse Relief petition with the IRS, explaining how everything had played out. Rebecca had done everything correctly by having the appropriate taxes withheld from her paycheck. Timothy had made estimated tax payments throughout the year following what he thought his income from the business had required, but it didn't include the income from the restaurant chain. As Rebecca had nothing to do with Timothy's business, she had no way of knowing that an error had occurred with his accounting. Under the Equitable Relief portion of the Innocent Spouse program, we got some of Rebecca's withholdings returned to her, but it took over four months to hammer through with the IRS.

Now, you must balance out the pros and cons of such a program before jumping into it. Remember that penalties and interest accrue on any unpaid tax. Yes, there are ways to get your properly paid tax overages back if your spouse makes an error on your joint tax return that you had no way of knowing occurred. However, if you plan to stay married to the person and continue to handle your household finances jointly, it may not be worth seeking the tax monies back.

Injured Spouse Relief Doesn't Refer to Getting a Black Eye from Tripping Down the Stairs

Picture this scenario: you are newly married, enjoying your first year of marital bliss, and come tax time, you proudly sign your first income tax return as a couple. With the joint financial picture reported on the return, you expect a tax refund of $6,500.00... yay! Visions of new furniture or a beach vacation dance in your head. Unfortunately, instead of getting a check for $6,500, you get a letter saying that the tax refund has been confiscated and applied to a past-due 1040 balance owed by your newly minted spouse. OUCH!

Believe it or not, this scenario is more common than one would expect or hope! Fear not, however, as the Injured Spouse Relief program is a way to handle the situation to protect the spouse who did not owe the past-due taxes.

Using this program, the spouse who did not have the tax debt can protect their interest in any refund owed by claiming a non-responsibility for the other's tax bill.

The best way to propose this to the IRS is by submitting the proper form as an attachment to the joint income tax return when it is first filed.

127

However, if you don't, there is still a way the non-responsible spouse can petition for this protection after the IRS confiscates the money. It's a more involved process because trying to pry money away from the IRS after it is in their coffers is tough, but it can be done!

State Asterisks That Come Into Play

Most states have similar programs to the ones offered by the IRS to help an innocent or injured spouse. However, if you reside in a community property state, the Innocent Spouse and Injured Spouse programs at the federal and state levels get a lot trickier. You can find the guidelines by searching the internet or contacting an experienced tax debt resolution professional (like me!) for help and guidance.

Summary

Just because you file a joint income tax return, it doesn't mean you always have to be equally responsible for a tax assessment, and you usually don't have to be accountable for a tax debt your spouse had from before you were married. Remember, there is *ALWAYS* a solution!

Chapter 17:

Is There a Limit to How Long the IRS Can Come After a Tax Debt?

The IRS cannot collect on a tax debt forever. It *will* come to an end. But know that this is where the IRS and a lot of states are divided because tax dollars are more like Monopoly money at the federal level than at the state level. Every tax dollar means more to your state than to the feds. I will refer to the IRS' collection timeframe in this book for simplicity's sake because every state has its own laws regarding how long they can chase a tax balance owed. If you want specific collection timeframes for your state, let your fingers do the walking on the internet or call the agency directly and ask.

First things first, once a tax debt is *recorded* on a tax account, a ten-year clock starts ticking. The IRS only has ten years to collect on each balance, and they look at these clocks separately for each year. The tax bill you accrue on your 2015 income tax return starts with a collection expiration date of April 2026 (remember they are filed in April of the following year if submitted on time!) or ten years from the date the return is processed if you submit it after the initial filing deadline.

However, there are some situations where the collection timeframe might be extended. Here are some examples:

- Filing bankruptcy
- Applying for an Offer in Compromise
- Responding to a notice received with a request for a Collection Due Process Hearing
- Requesting an Installment Agreement
- Being out of the country for longer than six months

- If you are serving in a combat zone

Essentially, if you took some action that prevented the IRS from being able to collect on the debt, this ten-year ticking clock gets paused.

Now, there are circumstances when your resolution plan is simply "waiting out the collection statutes" until the debt can be written off. I don't always recommend this as the best strategy because you still have exposure to any collection actions the IRS deems fit (tax refund seizure, bank account levies, Social Security levies, etc.). However, as I reviewed in the chapter on the Currently Not-Collectible strategy (Chapter 11), it is sometimes a viable option.

After ten years and under normal circumstances, the debt is written off, and any Federal Tax Lien filed will be removed.

A client was referred to me by his accountant, who had a situation that warranted us running the collection clock. Michael came to us in 2022 with a lingering tax debt from 2009 and 2010 that amounted to over $35,000 in past-due taxes owed to the IRS. He was retired and living primarily off his monthly Social Security benefits. He did have money from the settlement of a lawsuit two years prior that was being held in trust by his attorney, but he didn't want to access those funds until his taxes had been dealt with.

Upon contacting the IRS, I found that he had been placed into a Currently Not-Collectible Status in 2021, and there were only seven months left on the IRS' collection statute for the late-filed 2009 and 2010 tax returns.

After reviewing everything with Michael, we agreed to put our feet up on the corner of my desk and wait. For six months, we pulled his IRS account transcripts and monitored them for any signs of activity by the IRS. With a sigh of relief, we hit the magic collection statute expiration date, requested copies of the tax lien release records, and sent Michael on to enjoy the rest of his life free of any IRS concerns.

Summary

There is a statute of limitations for how long the IRS can chase you to pay a tax debt. Think of it as a fail-safe so you know the IRS will not keep hounding you for the rest of your life. We always use the collection statute expiration date as a puzzle piece when developing the best resolution plans for our clients. Sometimes, it is the deciding factor between setting up an Installment Agreement or petitioning for an Offer in Compromise. The good news is that if you have a tax debt, there is always an endpoint with the IRS. Remember, there is *ALWAYS* a solution!

Chapter 18:

When Should I Get a Tax Debt Professional Involved?

Deanna received a collection letter from the IRS for $958 triggered by a disallowed deduction. She called a local accountant, a colleague of mine, and asked about the charge. My colleague explained that it would take about three hours of work at $275 an hour to assess the self-prepared tax return and all the supporting documentation and that, in the end, she would probably still have to pay the $958. The accountant advised, "Deanna, just take it on the chin and pay it unless you want to handle the challenge yourself."

Though I'm sure this wasn't what Deanna wanted to hear, it was sound advice. Hiring a tax professional to get involved can be costly, depending on what needs to be done. You have to weigh the costs against the time you have available to try to handle it yourself, the knowledge you do or don't have about taxes, and the results that could be attained.

I can't tell you how many people have come to me and my firm asking for tax representation help when their situation doesn't truly warrant it. I send them on their way with some guidance about how to handle the problem on their own. I sleep better at night knowing my team and I are honest with clients about whether their situation warrants our involvement or not. Watch out for the predatorial tax debt resolution mills because they'll say you need them no matter what your circumstances are!

If you have a past-due income tax debt owed to the California Franchise Tax Board that is less than $15,000, you can handle calling and setting up a monthly payment arrangement on your own. Now, suppose that bill is $15,000, and you have several years of unfiled tax returns that you know will have balances owed. You should probably get an experienced tax debt resolution professional involved in that case.

If you have a business payroll tax that is slowly growing quarter by quarter, even if it is only $15,000, you should consider getting a tax debt resolution professional involved. Remember, with payroll taxes, there is a personal responsibility component that could wreak havoc on your household.

DIY Resolution Pitfalls

Dealing with the IRS and state over a past-due tax bill can be stressful. Depending on the mood of the agent who answers your call to the phone number listed on the last collection notice received, you will see sunshine and rainbows, or it will rain cats and dogs. If you happen to be met by rudeness or doom and gloom when discussing your tax account with them, simply hang up the phone, wait a few hours, and then call back. At the state level, there are hundreds of agents who answer the phone lines. At the federal level, there are thousands of agents. The odds of you calling back hours later and ending up with the same person are 0.001%.

Don't let them push you into agreeing to a solution that you know you won't be able to uphold. Push back! If you need to, ask to speak with a manager. If that doesn't work, ask to speak with the taxpayer advocate's office. Remember, you are being proactive in wanting to address your debt; some consideration should be given.

Talk to your accountant or CPA if you don't want to handle it. Though their specialty is focused on tax planning and filing tax returns, they can handle calling the IRS or state and setting up a simple Installment Agreement on your behalf. You will have to pay them to do it, but if the idea of calling the tax agencies makes you break out in a cold sweat, paying them for the peace of mind would be worth it.

Does Your CPA Want to Handle a $20,000+ Resolution?

Consider this: to truly know how to navigate through the collection, examination, and appeal departments of the IRS and states efficiently and effectively, and to understand how the resolution programs play out in all the different scenarios that can come about, it takes *years* of dedicated experience. You can't take a weekend-long crash course in handling tax debt and claim to be knowledgeable enough to represent clients before the federal government. (You wouldn't want an auto mechanic working on your 2015 Z06 Corvette engine if all they did to prepare was a weekend-long crash course, would you???)

Your accountant or CPA spends most of their time on the tax codes and laws related to income, investments, business financial activities, deductions allowed, special credits offered in certain circumstances, and all things related to individual and business tax returns. Unless your accountant or CPA is as brilliant as Albert Einstein, there is simply no possible way that they can be considered an expert in all areas of the tax world. There may be some out there, but not many!

As an Enrolled Agent, I am licensed to provide the same services as a CPA or accountant: tax advisement, tax return preparation, payroll processing, etc. However, I don't go near those services because I chose early in my career to *only* focus on tax debt resolution. I'll proudly display the Heisman Trophy of Tax Debt Resolution on my bookshelf, knowing that I worked hard to be one of the best because of the focus and dedication I have given to it over the last two-plus decades.

> **Note:** Most of my time is spent with clients, individuals, or businesses, who owe the IRS, state, or a combination of the two, $25,000 to $2,000,000. Getting a giant tax bill out of your life is where my experience and training come into play. The strategic planning that goes into resolving tax debt is not done on a whim... there are many pieces of the puzzle to consider and if it's not someone's only area of practice, crucial details could be overlooked.

If you find yourself in the crosshairs of the IRS or state for more than $15,000 or have not filed for two or three years, ask your CPA point blank, "Should I hire an expert?" Then, call me or someone with similar experience, tenure, and credentials.

The Underlying Benefits of Hiring a Reputable Tax Debt Professional

First, know that the IRS and state are relieved when a power of attorney for a reputable tax debt resolution professional is received. Over the decades, I have encountered the same revenue officers for different taxpayers, often years apart, because I have represented clients nationwide over the last twenty-four years. The first phone call after I send over my power of attorney is typically met with, "It has been quite a while since I've had a case with you... how have you been???" Yes, revenue officers truly do talk like that to the right people, even when a large tax bill is involved!

This is because I have always been respectful and friendly during my phone calls and interactions with the agents I deal with. Even though we are on opposite sides of the tax collection desk, and I am always very clear that I am seeking a solution to the tax debt with my client's best interest in mind, it doesn't mean we can't both approach the tax debt solution in a civilized, courteous, and even friendly manner.

You know the adage that you catch more bees with honey than vinegar? It is true... and these officers and agents remember me for it!

If you display that you know the tax codes and laws surrounding tax debt collection and approach the negotiations from a cooperative yet unyielding position while advocating for your client, you earn the agent's respect on the other side of the negotiation desk.

This is the benefit of utilizing an experienced and respected tax debt resolution professional to handle your tax account concerns.

Be Careful Who You Tie to Your Tax Account

When you are considering getting a tax debt professional involved, where do you start?

First, do your research. Make sure their professional credentials are checked out. If they are an Enrolled Agent, use the IRS' Enrolled Agent database to ensure their license is in good standing. If they are a CPA, check with your state's CPA directory for the same validation. If they are an attorney, check the state board's registry. You want to make sure the person holds an active license.

Check out their website, any blogs posted, and even their social media activities. You want someone with a working, intimate knowledge of your tax debt scenario. Suppose they declare on their website, "We can handle anything and everything having to do with tax debt," but upon further review, you find that none of their blogs or social media activities share details focused on tax debt situations. In that case, they probably aren't as experienced as they hold themselves to be.

Check for online reviews but remember that anyone can say anything in an online review without validation; sometimes, nothing can be done to address it. You can't please all the people all the time… there will always be that one client who expects the representative to wave a magic wand to make the debt go away, and nothing short of that will make them happy. And these tend to be the most vociferous with negative online reviews!

Look at all the reviews available, toss out consideration for the highest and most pro-representative, and toss out the lowest and ugliest… your truth will be found somewhere in the middle. And watch out for personal vendetta reviews, as those tend not to even be from valid clients... they could even be from a neighbor who hates the representative on a personal level over a barking dog issue.

Ask your accountant or CPA for advice if you need help making an initial assessment. Because they eat, sleep, and breathe the tax world, they can solidly assess the professional you are considering.

Last, get the potential tax debt resolution professional on the phone. Talk to them for a bit and think about whether this is someone you feel like you would like to work with. Did they ask you questions that felt appropriate? Did they express a focused interest in you, your situation, and what you were saying, or did they sound distracted? Were they forthcoming about the process they utilize when a new client comes on board? Trust your gut. Yes, people can sometimes float you with a good sales pitch... however, if you pay attention, you'll cut through the fluff and B.S.

What's the Process Typically Used When I Hire a Tax Debt Resolution Professional?

I can't speak for every tax debt resolution professional in the nation, but most will conduct some type of onboarding process. Whenever a new client reaches out to my firm, my team and I follow a protocol that ensures we are a good fit for the client and that the client will be a good fit for me, my team, and the services we offer:

Step one: We conduct an initial intake consultation. We typically spend 20-30 minutes on a phone call learning the basics of the potential client's situation. How the tax debt came about, which tax agencies are involved, and what the tax compliance record is.

Step two: If we determine that the situation warrants involving a tax debt professional, we discuss our investigation process and the related fees.

> **Note:** Nobody will give your case the attention and dedicated mental involvement needed if they don't have their time and expenses covered. It will cost you some initial money down, but it will be money well-spent if you hire a reputable tax debt resolution professional to assess your tax situation and outline the options that can resolve the debt owed.

The investigation process allows us to move on with steps three, four, and five.

Step three: We file a Power of Attorney document with the IRS and any applicable states with a tax debt or concern. By doing so, we can access all of the client's tax account records, including transcripts for current tax debts on record and any wage and income records reported, and confirm the filing and tax payment obligations outstanding.

A Power of Attorney document also allows us to negotiate a hold on any ongoing threats of collection actions (bank account levies, wage garnishments, income levies, or asset seizures). This provides some breathing room to focus on tax compliance, submitting any outstanding returns, and mapping out a resolution strategy.

Step four: We discuss the client's financial condition in detail. Suppose their tax debt problems are for personal tax obligations. In that case, we ask about what they do to earn income, marital/dependent status, average monthly income and expenses, and where they would like to be financially in five years. If it's a business tax debt, we learn about the company: history, typical income and expense levels, assets with significant equity held, potential impacts to the business that caused the debt, and where the client wants the company to be in five years.

Step five: We gather all this information into an Investigation Report. This report provides a clear summary of the debts owed, compliance issues that must be addressed, the top two or three resolution options available, and the time and costs associated with each option. Then, my team and I will call the client to discuss the entire report. We discuss the pros and cons of each resolution option, which option we believe best fits the client's case based on our decades of tax debt resolution experience, and address any questions or concerns the client has.

Step six: Once the client has decided which option they would like to proceed with, we finalize a contract for our continued representation and get to work.

Is It Expensive to Hire a Tax Debt Professional?

Of course, it is... but if you hire a reputable and experienced tax debt resolution professional, just the peace of mind of knowing that somebody is handling the situation for you as long as you follow their lead is worth its weight in gold.

At the time of this book's writing, the average hourly rate for a reputable tax debt resolution professional is between $250 and $600 per hour. That's a big swing... the difference usually being whether they are self-employed with one assistant or have an office in a high-rise building with glass walls full of administrative staff. My team and I are some of the best in the tax debt resolution industry, and we average in the middle. So budget accordingly if you have a tax debt owed.

Is it worth paying someone $9,000 to handle the tax debt, and you come out the other end keeping your home? I would say so. If you end up paying a tax debt professional $38,000 over two years to submit and negotiate an Offer in Compromise that results in you walking away from $200,000 in past-due taxes owed, is it worth it? Absolutely. I'd say that was a bargain.

Without an initial investigation into your specific tax debt situation, nobody can give you a proper estimate of how much time and expense is involved in solving your tax debt. That would be like calling your auto mechanic and asking how much it costs to fix a car that won't start. You will not get an answer because they don't know if the battery is dead, or the crankshaft sensor is broken; they will give you a price after they look at the car.

Just know that if you hire a reputable and experienced tax debt resolution professional to solve your past-due tax debt, your money will be well spent.

Summary

The real pain of dealing with the IRS is the fear of the unknown. They might swoop down and take everything you've worked for over the last ten years. The solutions are complicated on purpose; the IRS and states want to collect every dime they can get their hands on and will leverage dealing with someone who doesn't know everything that can and can't be done when collecting on a tax debt to get more.

When an experienced tax debt resolution professional stands up to the IRS on your behalf, you have a fighting chance to survive and eventually prosper after the ordeal is concluded. It will be over sooner than you fear. Remember, there is *ALWAYS* a solution.

Chapter 19:
A Final Word

This book contains a LOT of information about tax debts and options to resolve them. It's a lot for anybody to ingest, especially if finances and the tax world aren't your chosen profession.

If I could hope for one thing to stick with you above everything else shared in this book, it's that there is *ALWAYS* a solution to a tax debt problem. To get there, you simply have to start putting one foot in front of the other.

I've been in this industry for a long time. I've seen some situations that would scare the biggest, hairiest, ugliest monsters imaginable.

I've dealt with tax debts resulting from the most selfish embezzlement and theft acts a human can commit against another. I've had to jump in between soon-to-be ex-spouses who were threatening physical violence against the other, all due to the stress of a joint tax debt that needed to be handled. I've had to call 911 to have the police make an emergency wellness visit to a client who said they were going to commit suicide over their tax debt. I've had to console a new client who was sobbing on the phone with me over the payroll taxes their in-house bookkeeper accrued, then conveniently skipped town.

The situations I have heard about over the last twenty-four years are heartbreaking. They can tear apart your hope for humanity if you let them. What inspires my team and me to keep doing this work that has a long-lasting impact on our clients and their futures is that there is *ALWAYS* a solution. We are experts at identifying, proposing, and negotiating those solutions, no matter what our client's situation may be.

Nothing is better than the phone calls we encounter at the end of our negotiations. To be able to call a client we have been working with over the last year to say, "It's done... we got it. You are set up with the resolution, your savings are $XXX, and you will no longer have to fear the IRS," is a feeling that still gives me goosebumps. The clients are always thrilled beyond belief! I have had clients jump up and down, screaming, "YES!!!! Thank God!!!!" I have had grown men get choked up while saying an emphatic "THANK YOU!" I have had clients say they will never forget me and the impact I have had on their family's future.

That's why I do this. I know there is *ALWAYS* a solution, and I love being the one able to find it.

At any time while you are reading this book, feel free to email me with questions or your thoughts... I'd love to hear from you!

Morgan Q. Anderson, Enrolled Agent & NTPI Fellow

Morgan.Q.Anderson@GoldenLionTaxSolutions.com

www.goldenliontaxsolutions.com

Acknowledgments

Nobody gets to where they are in life alone… me included! I want to take a moment to acknowledge the following people. Each and every one of you has helped shape who I am today…

To Chris, Spencer, & Vivienne – I love you three more than I can express… our little family is more than I ever dreamed I would be blessed with. Thank you for being such an inspiration for everything I do and all the goals I have dreamed up for us. Monkey, you are the best partner a Chewy could be blessed with!

To my Dad and Mom – We made it! You have always been there for me and helped form my passion for always doing the right thing, even when it wasn't easy. You taught me to have a relentless work ethic and to always reach for the stars. I admire you both more than you could ever know, and I count my blessings for you every single day! Big salutes and great reverence for the Colonels!

To my Mom in heaven – I know you are jumping in and providing a guiding hand from the stars. I wouldn't be the person I am today without everything we went through!

To Harper and Jaime – Thank you for the lessons I learned as we navigated through being sisters. A lot of good, some bad, and some just plain ugly, but they helped us all form who we are today. May you and your families always be blessed with everything you need and have a passion for everything you do in life!

To my Uncle Tony, Aunt Jen Anne, Chris, Beth, and Aidan – The miles may separate us all, but I love the times when we can get together. There's nothing better than family, and I always come away from our visits with stitches in my side from the laughter!!! Uncle, I'm still holding out for my 60s muscle car, and Aunt Jen Anne, I still want the recipe for your chocolate cake! Aidan, swing for the stars!!!

To my Auntie Joy, Auntie Gay, Uncle Mark, and all the Kruszynski clan – So many memories and key moments in my life came from when we were together at the farm. Be-I and Grandmere laid the foundation for having the courage to build my own business. God bless LaFrance Manufacturing!

To my Anderson family - Thank you so much for welcoming me with open arms all those years ago. I love all of you and look forward to days when we can all spend more time together!

To my Cislaghi family - Thank you so much for being a part of our world and for the fun times we have been able to share!

To Matt Mulligan and Scott Priesmeyer – Thanks for taking a chance on a 25-year-old Nerinx girl with a brain but no real direction in life. I learned the foundations of the tax debt world within your offices and then ran with it. It was an honor to work with you both!

To Mariah – Thank you so much for taking a chance with me and GLTS. I can't wait to see how we continue to grow over the coming decades… there are thousands more clients we can help. It is a pleasure to do so with you right next to me! To the moon and the stars!!!! And Lylah, always follow your passion, and don't stop smiling!

To my StL girls and the Real Housewives of Westgate– Thank you so much for your friendship and support. We are all stronger for the shoulders we have provided to one another, our lives are more joyful for the laughter we have shared, and the tales we have amassed from our adventures will stick with me for the rest of my life. I love you all!

To Annie and Tony – "How many years has it been???" What a crazy path we have taken together since you answered that ad in St. Louis. It was divine intervention! I appreciate you both and love that we have endured all of life's curve balls together!!!

To Cheryl – My dear friend and biggest cheerleader, I still want to visit Graceland with you, as long as we don't end up behind bars singing "Jailhouse Rock," though there's nobody I would rather sing it with! And yes, Mariah, you better be there, too!

To Bill, Ingrid, and the team at bluedress – you all are the bomb-diggity!!! Thank you for helping create Rex and the path for Golden Lion to grow into my vision!

Last but certainly not least, I thank all the people who worked with me over the decades, especially those who endured as I learned how to manage employees and, more importantly, how NOT to manage employees. Thanks for riding the wave of the good times and sticking with me through the low times!

Made in United States
Troutdale, OR
11/05/2024

24469399R00096